Clothed in GLORY

Vesting the Church

Edited by **DAVID PHILIPPART**

LITURGY
TRAINING
PUBLICATIONS

ACKNOWLEDGMENTS

This book was designed by Carolyn Riege, Kerry Perlmutter and Lisa Buckley, typeset in Goudy Old Style by James Mellody-Pizzato, and printed by Thiessen Printing Corp. of Chicago, Illinois. David Philippart was the editor, and Deborah Bogaert was the production editor. The cover photo is of a textile by Catherine Kapikian.

All scripture citations are from the New Revised Standard Version of the Bible, copyright © 1989 by the Division of Christian Education of the National Council of Churches of Christ in the United States of America.

Excerpts from the English translation of the Rite of Baptism for Children © 1969, International Committee on English in the Liturgy, Inc. (ICEL); excerpts from the English translation of the Rite of Christian Initiation of Adults © 1985, ICEL. All rights reserved.

The commentaries on the vesting prayers in chapter five are from The Book of Ceremonies, by Rev. Laurence J. O'Connell. Milwaukee: Bruce Publishing Company, 1944, pp. 73 — 74.

The following chapters first appeared as articles in Environment & Art Letter, published monthly since March 1988 by Liturgy Training Publications:

"The Alb," by Ronald John Zawilla, April 1993; "Vesting the Coffin," originally published as "Christian Funeral Items," by Linda Schapper and David Philippart, November 1993; "Vesting the Ordained," originally published as "Vesture for the Ordained: The Chasuble, Dalmatic and Stole," by Ronald John Zawilla, July 1993; "The Cope," by Ronald John Zawilla, February 1994; "Textiles for the Church: A Primer," by Connie Cassani Beard, August 1989; "Banner Basics," by Judy Kensel Dioszegi, September 1991; "Hanging Banners and Mobiles," by John Dioszegi, January 1992; "Prayer Rugs," photos courtesy of the Art Institute of Chicago and Regina Kuehn, January 1995; "Learning from Laliberté," by Mark Scott, February 1994; "Working with a Weaver," by Lynn Lautz, September 1988; "Caring for the Church's Vesture," originally published in three parts as "Care of Liturgical Textiles," March 1990, "Textiles: Care and Storage," June 1990, and "Textiles: The Washable Ones," July 1990, by Mickey Wright.

"Vesting the Newly Baptized" first appeared as "Appendix Part Nine: Baptismal Garment Directions," in The Three Days, revised edition, by Gabe Huck, published by LTP in 1992.

"The Use of Liturgical Colors" is excerpted from chapter 22 and "The Altar Cloth and Other Linens," is excerpted from chapters 7 and 23 of The Sacristy Manual, by G. Thomas Ryan, published by LTP in 1993.

04 03 02 01 00 99 98 97   7 6 5 4 3 2 1

Clothed in glory : vesting the church / edited by David Philippart.
         p.   cm.
     1. Church vestments. I. Philippart, David.
   BV167.C56   1997
   247 — dc21   97-22691
                                                                                                         CIP

ISBN 1-56854-187-2
GLORY

CONTENTS

CLOTHED IN GLORY
The Human Body

You clothed me in skin and flesh,
and knit me together with bones and sinews.
You have granted me life and steadfast love,
and your care has preserved my spirit.

Job 10:11–12

So when the woman saw that the tree was good for food, and that it was a delight to the eyes, and that the tree was to be desired to make one wise, she took of its fruit and ate; and she also gave some to her husband, who was with her, and he ate. Then the eyes of both were opened, and they knew that they were naked; and they sewed fig leaves together and made loin-cloths for themselves.

Genesis 3:6 – 7

And the LORD made garments of skin for the man and for his wife, and clothed them.

Genesis 3:21

Joseph, being seventeen years old, was shepherding the flock with his brothers; he was a helper to the sons of Bilhah and Zilpah, his father's wives; and Joseph brought a bad report of them to their father. Now Israel loved Joseph more than any other of his children, because he was the son of his old age; and he had made him a long robe with sleeves.

Genesis 37:2 – 3

So when Joseph came to his brothers, they stripped him of his robe, the long robe with sleeves that he wore; and they took him and threw him into a pit.

Genesis 37:23

When Reuben returned to the pit and saw that Joseph was not in the pit, he tore his clothes. He returned to his brothers, and said, "The boy is gone; and I, where can I turn?" Then they took Joseph's robe, slaughtered a goat, and dipped the robe in the blood. They had the long robe with sleeves taken to their father, and they said, "This we have found; see now whether it is your son's robe or not." He recognized it, and said, "It is my son's robe! A wild animal has devoured him; Joseph is without doubt torn to pieces." Then Jacob tore his garments, and put sackcloth on his loins, and mourned for his son many days.

Genesis 37:29 – 34

And Pharaoh said to Joseph, "See I have set you over all the land of Egypt." Removing his signet ring from his hand, Pharaoh put it on Joseph's hand; he arrayed him in garments of fine linen, and put a gold chain around his neck.

Genesis 41:41 – 42

Joseph gave the sons of Israel wagons according to the instruction of Pharaoh, and he gave them provisions for the journey. To each one of them he gave a set of garments.

Genesis 45:21 – 22

The Lord said to Moses: "You shall make sacred vestments for the glorious adornment of your brother Aaron. And you shall speak to all who have ability, whom I have adorned with skill, that they make Aaron's vestments to consecrate him for my priesthood. These are the vestments that they shall make: a breastpiece, an ephod, a robe, a checkered tunic, a turban, and a sash. When they make these sacred vestments for your brother Aaron and his sons to serve me as priests, they shall use gold, blue, purple and crimson yarns, and fine linen."

Exodus 28:2 – 5

The Lord said to Moses: "You shall make the robe of the ephod all of blue. It shall have an opening for the head in the middle of it, with a woven binding around the opening, like the opening in a coat of mail, so that it may not be torn. On its lower hem you shall make pomegranates of blue, purple and crimson yarns, all around the lower hem, with bells of gold between them all around — a golden bell and a pomegranate alternating all around the lower hem of the robe. Aaron shall wear it when he ministers, and its sound shall be heard when he goes into the holy place before the LORD, and when he comes out, so that he may not die."

Exodus 28:31 – 35

Judith remained as a widow for three years and four months at home where she set up a tent for herself on the roof of her house. She put sackcloth around her waist and dressed in widow's clothing. She fasted all the days of her widowhood, except the day before the sabbath and the sabbath itself, the day before the new moon, and the day of the new moon, and the festivals and days of rejoicing of the house of Israel. She was beautiful in appearance, and was very lovely to behold.

Judith 8:4 – 7

When Judith had stopped crying out to the God of Israel, and had ended all these words, she rose from where she lay prostrate. She called her maid and went down into the house where she lived on sabbaths and on her festal days. She removed the sackcloth she had been wearing, took off her widow's garments, bathed her body with water, and anointed herself with precious ointment. She combed her hair, put on a tiara, and dressed herself in the festive attire that she used to wear while her husband

Manasseh was alive. She put sandals on her feet, and put on her anklets, bracelets, rings, earrings, and all her other jewelry.

Judith 10:1–4

Then Queen Esther, seized with deadly anxiety, fled to the Lord. She took off her splendid apparel and put on garments of distress and mourning.

Esther 14:1

On the third day, when she ended her prayer, Queen Esther took off the garments in which she had worshiped, and arrayed herself in splendid attire. Then, majestically adorned, after invoking the aid of the all-seeing God and Savior, she took two maids with her; on one she leaned gently for support, and the other followed, carrying her train. She was radiant with perfect beauty, and looked happy, as if beloved.

Esther 15:1–5

I will greatly rejoice in the LORD,
　my whole being shall exult in my God;
for he has clothed me with the garments of salvation,
　he has covered me with the robe of righteousness,
as a bridegroom decks himself with a garland,
　and as a bride adorns herself with her jewels.

Isaiah 61:10

She seeks wool and flax,
　and works with willing hands.
She is like the ships of the merchant,
　she brings her food from far away.
She rises while it is still night
　and provides food for her household
　and tasks for her servant-girls.
She considers a field and buys it:
　with the fruit of her hands she plants a vineyard.
She girds herself with strength
　and makes her arms strong.

She perceives that her merchandise is profitable.
　　Her lamp does not go out at night.
She puts her hands to the distaff,
　　and her hands hold the spindle.
She opens her hand to the poor,
　　and reaches out her hands to the needy.
She is not afraid for her household when it snows,
　　for all her household are clothed in crimson.
She makes herself coverings:
　　her clothing is fine linen and purple.
She makes linen garments and sells them;
　　she supplies the merchant with sashes.
Strength and dignity are her clothing,
　　and she laughs at the time to come.
She opens her mouth with wisdom,
　　and the teaching of kindness is on her tongue.

Proverbs 31:13 – 22, 24 – 26

While they were there, the time came for Mary to deliver her child. And she gave birth to her firstborn son and wrapped him in bands of cloth, and laid him in a manger.

Luke 2:6

Jesus took with him Peter and James and John, and led them up a high mountain apart, by themselves. And he was transfigured before them, and his clothes became dazzling white, such as no one on earth could bleach them.

Mark 9:2 – 3

And during supper Jesus, knowing that the Father had given all things into his hands, and that he had come from God and was going to God, got up from the table, took off his outer robe, and tied a towel around himself. Then he poured water into a basin and began to wash the disciples' feet and to wipe them with the towel that was wrapped around him.

John 13:2 – 5

Then Pilate took Jesus and had him flogged. And the soldiers wove a crown of thorns and put it on his head, and they dressed him in a purple robe.

John 19:1–2

When the soldiers had crucified Jesus, they took his clothes and divided them into four parts, one for each soldier. They also took his tunic; now the tunic was seamless, woven in one piece from the top. So they said to one another, "Let us not tear it, but cast lots for it to see who will get it." This was to fulfill what the scriptures says,

"They divided my clothes among themselves,
and for my clothing they cast lots."

John 19:23–24

Then Joseph bought a linen cloth, and taking down the body, wrapped it in a linen cloth, and laid it in a tomb that had been hewn out of the rock.

Mark 15:46

As they entered the tomb, they saw a young man, dressed in a white robe, sitting on the right side; and they were alarmed.

Mark 16:5

As God's chosen ones, holy and beloved, clothe yourselves with compassion, kindness, humility, meekness and patience. Bear with one another and, if anyone has a complaint against another, forgive each other; just as the Lord has forgiven you, so you also must forgive. Above all, clothe yourself with love, which binds everything together in perfect harmony.

Colossians 3:12–14

A great portent appeared in heaven: a woman clothed with the sun, with the moon under her feet, and on her head a crown of twelve stars.

Revelation 12:1

I looked, and there was a great multitude that no one could count, from every nation, from all tribes and peoples and languages, standing before the throne and before the Lamb, robed in white, with palm branches in their hands.

Revelation 7:9

Then one of the elders addressed me, saying, "Who are these, robed in white, and where have they come from?" I said to him, "Sir, you are the one that knows." Then he said to me, "These are they who have come out of the great ordeal; they have washed their robes and made them white in the blood of the Lamb.

For this reason they are before the throne of God,
and worship him day and night within his temple,
and the one who is seated on the throne
    will shelter them.
They will hunger no more and thirst no more;
the sun will not strike them,
nor any scorching heat;
for the Lamb at the center of the throne will be their shepherd,
and he will guide them to the springs of the water of life,
and God will wipe away every tear from their eyes."

Revelation 7:13–18

Then I heard what seemed to be the voice of a great multitude, like the sound of many waters and like the sound of mighty thunder peals, crying out,
Hallelujah!
For the Lord our God
    the Almighty reigns.
Let us rejoice and exult,
    and give him the glory
for the marriage of the Lamb has come
    and his bride has made herself ready:
to her it has been granted to be clothed
    with fine linen, bright and pure —
for the fine linen is the righteous deeds of the saints.

Revelation 19:6–8

THE ALB

Ronald John Zawilla

Liturgical vesture, like everyday clothing, evolves as part of a culture and is affected somewhat by notions of fashion. But until the twentieth century, the seasons of liturgical fashion were measured in centuries rather than in years. Great changes in liturgical vesture have occurred in the twentieth century for two reasons. First, the liturgical movement of the late nineteenth and early twentieth centuries promoted a return to forms of vesture from the early Christian and medieval periods. Second, the reforms of the Second Vatican Council simplified the required vesture, sparking new designs and changing the ways in which vesture was used.

The history of Christian vesture is a key to understanding its purpose, and it provides the proper context in which to discuss practical issues of form, fabric and construction. In this section we will sketch the history of Christian vesture and examine the alb, the basic Christian vestment, as a sign of the priesthood of the baptized.

THE ALB AS CLOTHING

In Christian antiquity, the vesture of the presider and ministers at liturgy was the same as that of the assembly: their everyday clothing. This remained true until the fifth and sixth centuries, when the forms of everyday clothing changed rather dramatically with the heavy influx of foreigners into the Western Roman Empire. Although styles of clothing changed, Christian ministers retained the forms of liturgical vesture that time and continuous use had hallowed. The notion of having sacred vesture that was distinct in form from everyday vesture was born as the old forms were endowed with symbolic meaning.

But from the beginning, the garments worn by presiders and other ministers at liturgy were special, not because they were different in style from everyday clothing but because they were set apart for exclusive use in liturgical celebrations. What we call the alb was then simply a white tunic (*alb* is Latin for "white") worn by men and women in slightly different forms as their basic garment. Generally, another garment, either a *pallium*, *dalmatica* or *casula*, also called a *paenula* or *planeta*, was worn over the tunic. These various forms of outer garment gave us, in time, the dalmatic and chasuble.

Before it became a distinctive liturgical garment, the alb — called a *tunica* or *colobium* — was shaped somewhat like a pillowcase with openings for the head and arms. It had no sleeves, although the ample width of the garment fell over the shoulders, covering the upper arms almost to the elbows. Laborers and servants wore knee-length tunics that allowed them ample freedom of movement, while people of the upper classes wore ankle-length tunics (*tunica talaris*). The *tunica talaris* was thus a kind of status symbol because its length inhibited manual labor. All tunics were worn with belts (*cingula*), by means of which the length could be regulated.

Tunics were made of wool or linen, or occasionally of cotton. Around the middle of the third century, a new fabric was introduced: semi-silk (*subserica*), a blend of silk with cotton or wool. Tunics were most often made from a single piece of fabric folded at the shoulder, with the sides stitched together and an opening cut for the head. Tunics frequently were decorated with vertical stripes (*claves*) indicating the class or rank of the wearer.

At a later period, the tunic was decorated with round or rectangular pieces of embroidered fabric (*segmenta*). Toward the end of the third century, sleeves were added to the originally sleeveless tunic. Although sleeves could be attached to the pillowcase form, the tunic was usually made instead in the shape of a large "T" cut from a single, folded piece of cloth.

THE ALB AS SYMBOL

For the early Christians, the symbolism of vesture derived not from its shape, form or style but from its newness or oldness and its cleanness or dirtiness. (The garb worn by members of orders of penitents was distinctive: Although it was a tunic like that worn by everyone else, it was soiled — deliberately — with ashes.) There was a belief in the ancient world that clothing becomes charged with the spiritual forces that surround the wearer. Special clothing was required to safeguard the purity of a sacred place. For Christians, who, strictly speaking, did not worship in sacred places, the newness of the garments signified something else, namely, the newness of life received in baptism and mediated in the celebration of the mysteries.

The garment signified the restoration of the robe of grace that clothed Adam and Eve before the fall. Patristic writers believed that Adam and Eve's discovery that they were naked (Genesis 3:7) implied that previously they had been clothed. In sinning, they had actually been stripped of divine grace, which they had worn like a robe. When God expelled Adam and Eve from paradise, God fashioned for them garments of animal skins, signifying their mortality.

At baptism, the catechumen was first stripped of his or her clothing, signifying the stripping of the old, sinful, mortal self. This stripping was as important symbolically as the vesting. After emerging from the font, the neophyte was clothed in a new white robe, signifying the putting on of Christ, who triumphed over death. In baptism the Christian becomes a new creation, remade in the image of Christ. Saint Paul says, "You have put off the old nature with its practices and have put on the new nature, which is being renewed in knowledge after the image of its creator" (Colossians 3:9–10).

The white robe therefore signifies the purity of the soul and the resurrection of the body. Patristic writers occasionally make reference to the Transfiguration, when Christ's robes shined with the light of the resurrection (Matthew 17:2). "The one who is baptized," says Saint Ambrose, "is pure, according to the gospel, because the garments of Christ were white as snow when, in the gospel, he showed forth the glory of his resurrection" (*De mysteriis* 34).

In the Book of Revelation, those participating in the heavenly liturgy are clothed in white. The image was probably drawn from the liturgy the author knew at the time Revelation was written. The 24 elders "clad in white garments" surround the throne (Revelation 4:4). The martyrs, "those who had been slain for the word of God," were given a white garment to wear (Revelation 6:9–11). Finally, there is the vision of the elect, "from every nation, from all tribes, peoples and tongues, standing before the Lamb, clothed in white robes, with palm branches in their hands and crying with a loud voice, 'Salvation belongs to our God who sits upon the throne and to the Lamb'" (Revelation 7:9–10). The white garments of those who participate in the heavenly liturgy symbolize the resurrection of the flesh.

Perhaps also contributing to the early Christian symbolism of the alb was the fact that the robes of the high priest in the Jerusalem Temple were of white linen. Though patristic writers make no overt connection between the baptismal garment and priestly vesture, baptism is a share in the priesthood of Christ: "You are a chosen race, a royal priesthood, a holy nation, God's own people" (1 Peter 2:9).

FROM BAPTISMAL GARMENT TO CLERICAL VESTMENT

In the Middles Ages, as the number of adult converts diminished relative to the number of infant baptisms, the significance of the baptismal garment diminished. In fact, it seems as if its symbolism was transferred to the alb, which became a liturgical vestment for clerics only. Early medieval writers, usually without referring to baptism, nonetheless attribute to the alb of the clerics the symbolism of purity of heart and soul.

In his very influential commentary on the liturgy, Pope Innocent III discusses the symbolism of the alb, equating the alb with the baptismal garment:

> The alb is a linen vestment, far removed from the tunic made of the skins of dead animals with which Adam was clothed after sin, signifying the newness of life that Christ had taught, and bestowed in baptism, about which the Apostle Paul says: "Put off the old nature with its acts and put on the new, created in the likeness of God." (*De sacro altaris mysterio* I.36 [PL 217.787–788])

In the Middle Ages the alb underwent some changes. The sleeves were made narrower, while the skirt was made fuller. The surplice (superpellicium), as a modification of the alb, appeared in the eleventh century as a choir garment worn over the black habits of canons and monks. In the thirteenth and fourteenth centuries the surplice gradually came to be used by priests in the celebration of the sacraments and by the lower ranks of clergy. Medieval surplices were of generous shape; they reached to the ankles and had very wide sleeves.

USING ALBS TODAY

In Christian antiquity, the white baptismal garment and the special white robe set aside for liturgical use by presiders and ministers at the altar were the same in origin and in meaning. In effect, Christian ministers wore their baptismal garments when exercising their offices. This became even more evident when the tunic ceased to be worn as everyday clothing but was retained as liturgical vesture. The alb, then, is the garb of all those who, through baptism, share in the priesthood of Christ.

The wearing of the white garment by adults at their baptism, the wearing of albs by ministers at the altar, and the wearing of the alb by ordained ministers (even though they wear it underneath other vesture) speaks of the rootedness of liturgical ministry in baptism. This was very clear a few years ago in the celebration of the Easter Vigil at St. Francis Xavier Church in St. Louis. The acolytes, ministers and presider all wore albs of like design — fully cut and free-flowing. At the moment when the newly baptized were clothed in the baptismal robes, the picture became complete. They were given robes of the same design as those worn by the ministers.

That image conveyed clearly the idea that the baptized are a priestly people in Christ, sharing in his priesthood through baptism and called to minister to one another. The alb is the baptismal robe, the garb of the people; it is not clerical vesture. The use of the alb visually bridges the gap between clergy and laity and reminds us that all ministry is rooted in baptism.

There is sometimes a reluctance to vest lay people when they serve as cantors, readers or acolytes. The reason usually given is that vestments are clerical. That was certainly true when we dressed small boys in cassocks and surplices. But the alb is the vestment of the faithful; it is the baptismal garment. When ordained ministers wear the alb it is in affirmation of their baptismal dignity and their oneness with those whom they serve. What they put on over the alb signifies their particular ministry in the community. When the baptized put on the alb to minister in the liturgy, it becomes clear that they are there by virtue of their baptism.

The environment for worship should embody and proclaim what the assembly believes. The visual is very important, but it speaks more softly than words — and it often speaks more profoundly. Such was the experience at St. Francis Xavier Church in St. Louis, where the community commissioned 25 albs in various sizes. The design — ample, simple, elegant and practical — is a large "T" shape with an opening for the head and a high, stand-up, rolled collar. Similar to a loose turtleneck, the collar is comfortable and hides whatever is worn underneath. These albs can be worn equally well by both women and men.

The simpler the design of the alb, the better. Excessive tailoring, pleating and the like never achieve the same nobility as a straightforward pattern. The beautiful garments of Africa, the flowing caftan of the Arab world and the clothing of the West in late antiquity offer the best models.

A concern sometimes raised is that wide sleeves will knock over vessels on the altar. Another concern is that ministers will trip wearing long, full garments. It takes a little practice to wear garments that are unlike everyday clothes. And movement in liturgy should be relaxed and deliberate, not fast and "efficient." Gracious vesture promotes gracious movement.

A proper-fitting alb is about ankle-length. Looking down at your feet while wearing an alb makes it appear longer than it is when you are standing up straight and looking ahead. There is no need to use a cincture as a belt if your alb fits properly. Nothing looks sloppier than the uneven hemline of a cinctured alb. Part of the alb's beauty is its free-flowing graciousness. Using a cincture therefore decreases the vestment's beauty.

I made the albs for the St. Louis community of a synthetic fabric, but I have since made an interesting discovery: raw silk. Raw silk noil is relatively inexpensive. Washing the fabric before cutting it prevents shrinkage later and allows the alb to be washed instead of dry cleaned. Putting it through the washer and dryer fluffs the fiber and brings out the nubbiness of the fabric. It looks heavy but flows and drapes exquisitely. It is opaque enough that even vibrantly colored clothing worn underneath will not be visible. What is perhaps more important, though, is that it is cool (natural fibers breathe) and resistant to wrinkles.

My suggestion, which at first may not seem very practical, is that a parish give each newly baptized adult an alb of the type described above. Those adults who minister at liturgy could also be given their own albs. This way, each would have an alb that fits properly, and there would be no worry about having five medium-height ministers at a given celebration and only four medium-sized albs. The ministers would care for their own albs, which would save a lot of work for someone else. And it would be a lovely custom to bury Christians in their baptismal robes.

The spirit of the reformed liturgy and the lessons learned from the renewed rites of Christian initiation affirm the dignity of the baptized as members of the body of Christ. What better way to incarnate this than through the careful use of beautifully designed albs for the newly baptized and for those who have a particular ministry in the liturgy?

VESTING THE NEWLY BAPTIZED

Judy Kensel Dioszegi

This pattern for a baptismal garment assumes that the work will be undertaken by an experienced person. The alb is designed to be enveloping. Sleeves should be full, and the garment should be long — to the lower calf or ankle.

Make a paper pattern first (perhaps using brown wrapping paper). Adjustments and size differences can be worked out on this paper pattern.

This design fits an average-to-large person comfortably. For smaller people, reduce the neckline by one-half inch and proportion the hem and the sleeve length accordingly.

One garment requires three yards of 60-inch-wide linen/polyester blend in white.

INSTRUCTIONS

Cut pattern according to diagram.

Fold fabric in half as indicated.

Smooth fabric and pin together sides.

Place paper pattern on fabric, and pin in position.

It may be easier to sew to shoulder seam first and then cut away.

Finish all raw edges.

Seam at ⅝ inch.

If a larger neck opening is required, enlarge from opening by ½ inch, as indicated by the dotted line.

Finish neckline with a narrow hem or a simple binding applied to the inside turned edge.

Sew lower edge of sleeves.

Bar-tack or straight-stitch at corner of sleeve and side seam for reinforcement. Clip corner to ease the fit.

Turn sides back ½ inch and stitch at ¼ inch.

Make necessary adjustments for sleeve and hem length.

Turn both back 1 inch and stitch at ¾ inch.

Press well.

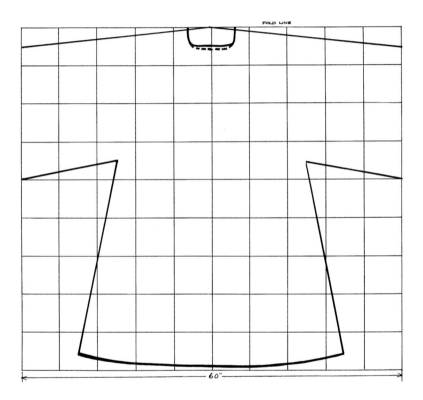

FOR FURTHER REFLECTION

214. Explanatory Rites: The baptismal washing is followed by rites that give expression to the effects of the sacrament just received. The anointing with chrism is a sign of the royal priesthood of the baptized and that they are now numbered in the company of the people of God. The clothing with the baptismal garment signifies the new dignity they have received. The presentation of the lighted candle shows that they are called to walk as befits children of the light.

Clothing with a Baptismal Garment

229. The garment used in this rite may be white or of a color that conforms to local custom. If circumstances suggest, this rite may be omitted.

The celebrant says the following formulary, and at the words "receive this baptismal garment," the godparent or godparents place the garment on the newly baptized.

N., you have become a new creation
and have clothed yourself with Christ.
Receive this baptismal garment
and bring it unstained to the judgment seat
    of our Lord Jesus Christ,
so that you may have everlasting life.

Newly baptized: Amen.

RITE OF CHRISTIAN INITIATION OF ADULTS

99. The celebrant says:

N., you have become a new creation
and have clothed yourself in Christ.
See in this white garment
the outward sign of your Christian dignity.
With your family and friends to help you
by word and example,
bring that dignity unstained
into the everlasting life of heaven.

All: Amen.

The white garment is put on the child. A different color is not permitted unless demanded by local custom. It is desirable that the family provide the garment.

RITE OF BAPTISM OF CHILDREN

Local customs will determine what robe (called *chrisom* is some liturgical traditions) is provided for adult neophytes and for children of catechetical age. Parishes should give priority to the alb. It is the basic garment of all liturgical ministers, as well as the traditional baptismal garment. Albs are readily available from many suppliers. If the neophytes keep their robes after taking them off at the end of the Vigil, the expense might be borne by special donors.

For the baptism of infants, many communities have experimented with little white items, some looking like bibs, others like stoles, many with insipid decoration. But most parents dress their infants for the occasion in wonderful christening dresses passed on from generation to generation. These are the baptismal garments, not the bibs. If there will be immersion baptism, then the baby can be wrapped in 'swaddling clothes' until the baptism and vested in the gown after. If families are unable to provide white garments like this, then a special group of parish members might be able to provide gowns that carry on the wonderfully full tradition of flowing, white vesture.

G. Thomas Ryan, *The Sacristy Manual*

In Easter week, in or around the year 335, Cyril, the bishop of Jerusalem, preached daily on the meaning of the rites of initiation celebrated the Saturday before. Here are excerpts from those homilies:

Stripping   Upon entering you took off your clothing, and this symbolized your stripping off of 'the old nature with its practices.' Stripped naked, in this too, you were imitating Christ naked on the cross, who in his darkness 'disarmed the principalities and the powers' and on the wood of the cross publicly 'triumphed over them.' Since hostile powers lurked in your limbs, you can no longer wear your former clothing; I do not of course refer to visible apparel but to 'your old nature which is corrupt through deceitful lusts.' I pray that the soul which has once thrown off that old nature may never resume it, but rather speak the words of Christ's bride in the Song of Songs: 'I had put off my garment; how could I put it on?' This was a remarkable occasion, for you stood naked in the sight of all and you were not ashamed. You truly mirrored our first-created parent Adam, who stood naked in Paradise and was not ashamed.

The Baptismal Garment   It is for this reason, to hint at this gift, that Solomon says in Ecclesiastes: 'Come then, eat your bread with enjoyment' — he means spiritual bread. 'Come then' — his invitation brings salvation and blessedness. 'And drink your wine with a merry heart' — the wine of the spirit. 'And let oil be poured over your head' — you see him here hinting also at the sacramental anointing. 'And let your garments always be white, because the Lord approved what you do.' For before you drew near to the gift, your works were 'vanity of vanities.'

Once you have stripped off the old garments and put on those that are spiritually white, you must be clad in white always. I am not of course saying that you must always wear white clothing on your body, but that your spiritual dress must be truly shining, so that you may say, in the words of blessed Isaiah: 'Let my soul rejoice in the Lord: he has clothed me with the garment of salvation, and with the robe of gladness he has covered me.'

VESTING THE COFFIN

Linda Schapper and David Philippart

Contemporary culture operates out of a tremendous fear of death that amounts to denial. Mark Twain remarked that you can tell a lot about a community by the funerals it holds. What do contemporary Christian funeral practices reveal about what we believe death to be? Does our ritual treatment of the body of a dead Christian show our respect for that member of the church? Does it reveal our belief in the resurrection of the body and in eternal life?

More than half of all deaths in the United States now occur in hospitals rather than at home. The body of the deceased is placed in an ornate metal coffin foreign in its materials and design to anything used in daily life and lined with fabrics not seen since the day of the senior prom. Then the body lies in state in a professional funeral home, where it may be viewed at certain times and is otherwise left unattended in a locked room. (At one point in our history — and it is still the practice in some other countries — wakes were held at home.)

At church, the coffin is covered with a pall made in some distant commercial factory, of some indestructible synthetic material guaranteed not to wrinkle, stain or burn. Furthermore, the pall is most often covered with poorly executed symbols — visual clichés not questioned or renewed and thus incapable of moving people.

SIMPLE THINGS

Christ came as a simple carpenter to show us that simple things —
a hand-crafted wood coffin, a handsewn pall and sturdy lyrics
sung to plain melodies, for example — have the power to carry
our spirits in times of painful uncertainty. It may take decades
for the churches to begin to reform society's denial of death, but
the parish can begin by examining how it enacts funeral rites.

The parish can resolve to take seriously the three-part
approach (vigil, funeral, committal) of the *Order of Christian
Funerals* (OCF), provide for singing in all the rites, insist that
cemeteries and funeral directors allow for graveside committal
rites and work toward providing a comprehensive bereavement
ministry. Those responsible for the worship environment can
participate in this renewal by offering alternatives and making
simple changes in funeral accessories: the coffin, the pall and
works of visual art (banners or icons in the funeral home or
church, or the Christian symbols — book of gospels, Bible, or
cross — that may be placed on the coffin at the start of the
liturgy; see OCF, 163.)

THE COFFIN

Different municipalities have different laws, but most legal
requirements for burial are satisfied by a sturdy wood coffin. If a
local carpenter is able and willing to make simple coffins, perhaps that information could be shared with the parish at large
so that people know that it is an option at the time of death.
Perhaps funeral directors may be willing to have a prototype on
display and act as the carpenter's agent. Those living near Amish
communities can research the possibility of purchasing Amish
coffins, which even today must be made of wood. Depending on
the particular Amish community, the coffin may be unvarnished,
varnished or painted; the interior may be completely bare or
finished with a lining made of white cotton batting. In any case,
it is plain — no satin tufting, no pillows, no decorations — and
befitting Christian burial. Wood comes from a tree — the tree
in the center of Eden lost to us in sin and the tree of life in the
middle of the new Jerusalem: The wood of the Christian's coffin
evokes the wood of the cross.

PLACING CHRISTIAN SYMBOLS

If it is parish custom to place Christian symbols on the coffin at
the start of the funeral, perhaps the family of the deceased could
be encouraged to use a cross and/or a Bible that belonged to the
deceased or is part of the family treasure. If the custom of placing

a cross or crucifix in the lid of the open coffin for the duration of the wake is practiced, perhaps a suitable one could be available for purchase (or given to the family as a gift) from the parish office. Or perhaps someone could work with the funeral director to see that a fitting cross or crucifix is available — something more appropriate than those ubiquitous skimpy bronze crosses with oversized corpuses.

ICONS AND TAPESTRIES

Other works of visual art may aid people in grieving and help strengthen their faith in Christ's victory over death. Two traditional images from Christian iconography concerning death are that of Christ the Good Shepherd (painted on the walls of various early Christian catacombs) and that of the heavenly Jerusalem (see especially the Book of Revelation). This last image is essentially one of home and of homecoming: "In my Father's house there are many rooms. . . . And when I go and prepare a place for you, I will come again and take you to myself, that where I am you may also be" (John 14:2 – 3). The parish may want to commission an icon or a tapestry of one of these images that can be placed in the room where the body is waked.

THE PALL

Although the placing of the pall on the coffin is optional in the OCF, its nearly universal use in this country indicates that it is a significant ritual and that a pall can be a significant symbol. A pall made especially for (maybe even by) a parish or one made and used as a family heirloom can be an effective sign of reverence for the dead and of faith in the eternal life promised in baptism. In the OCF, the pall is placed on the coffin in silence, but in the former rite, the words that accompanied the action linked the pall with the baptismal garment. (And just as the white robe is donned after the water baptism, so too in the OCF is the pall placed after the body is sprinkled with holy water.) Because of its link with the baptismal garment, and probably because of the post – Vatican II tradition of using white vesture for ministers of the funeral Mass, the pall most often is white. This is not required, however, and since the chasuble and dalmatic may be purple or black as a sign of penitence or sorrow, the pall might incorporate these or other colors as well. When I make palls, I often use gold accents and various shades of colors to show motion that may evoke the waters of baptism, the passing over from death to new life and/or the journey into light.

Because the pall is itself a symbol, and because the OCF allows for placing the gospel book, a Bible and/or a cross atop the coffin, there is no need to apply symbols to the pall. It is better to concentrate on colors, form and materials.

A quilted pall is a good idea for several reasons. The quilt is traditionally a sign of humility and has its origins in immigrants reusing what little they had by piecing together fragments from everyone's unused garments. Not only does the material for a quilt come from various members of the community, it is traditionally crafted communally, too. So the quilt in our culture is a symbol of communal care and mutual support.

A soft cotton or linen quilt enfolding and protecting the body of a deceased Christian evokes the care of the Good Shepherd and the warmth and care that characterizes the new Jerusalem. The pieced-together patches symbolize the casting off of old clothes in order to don something new. And the variety of pieces sewn together suggests something of the communion of saints — the interrelatedness of persons dead and living.

It would be a great gesture of pastoral care if gifted parishioners could design and sew the parish pall. But good intentions never replace artistry and skill. The dignity of the deceased Christian and the solemnity of the funeral rites require that the pall be technically perfect. Such an important requirement also suggests that it is not practical for a quilted pall to be made from old material scraps but rather from carefully selected, natural material.

Last year, tired after months of 18-hour days piecing together a quilted pall that a parish had commissioned, I drove over to attend a funeral in a community for which I had made another pall. It was a tragic situation — the funeral was at a Catholic high school for a 16-year-old. As I watched some students lovingly drape the pall over their friend, the words from the former funeral rite came to me, and for the first time I understood what they meant: "On the day of your baptism, you put on Christ. In the day of Christ's coming, may you be clothed with glory."

VESTING THE ORDAINED

Ronald John Zawilla

In a previous chapter, I discussed the liturgical vesture common to all ministers in the church. Here, I would like to discuss the vesture reserved for the ordained ministries: the chasuble, dalmatic and stole. I will survey the origin and development of these vestments, their forms and colors, and then offer some practical considerations.

ORIGINS

Like the alb, the vesture of the clerical orders originated and developed from the ordinary garments worn by the men and women of late antiquity. At first, there was no distinction in form or style between the vesture worn by ministers and that worn by other members of the assembly. What distinguished the garb of the ministers was that theirs was set aside specifically for liturgical use.

In the Greco-Roman world, an outer garment of some sort was normally worn over the tunic. The *pallium* was a rectangle of cloth three times as long as it was wide, usually about six by eighteen feet. One end of the *pallium* was draped over the left arm, the longer end went around the back, and the excess crossed over the front of the person and hung down over the left shoulder. Sometimes it was folded over lengthwise, becoming in the process a band about one foot wide and draped about the body with one end hanging down in front, the other down in back with both ends crossing over the left shoulder.

The other common outer garment was the *paenula*, which was made from a semicircle of cloth, open in the front and buttoned at the neck. There were two other versions of the *paenula*: the *planeta*, which was fuller (two-thirds of a circle), and the *casula*, which was less full (one-third of a circle).

Another outer garment that came into common use in the third century was the dalmatica, introduced into the West from Dalmatia in the 190s — at which time it was considered somewhat decadent. The *dalmatic* was simply a more ample tunic with wider sleeves than usual. It was frequently decorated with vertical bands down the front and back as well as on the sleeves.

Another common article of clothing was the *superhumerale*, later known as the *amictus*. It was a rectangle of cloth with two cords fastened to the ends of one of its longer sides, which was worn over the shoulders and fixed with the cords that wrapped around the back and tied in the front. The *superhumerale* was worn under the outer garment, and its purpose was to fill in the neck opening. The *sudarium*, a kind of large handkerchief, was worn about the neck or over one shoulder. *Oraria* were rectangular cloths first mentioned as having been given by the emperor Aurelian to those who attended the public games, to be used to signal their approval or disapproval of the proceedings. Servants used their *oraria* to wipe vessels and perform other, similar tasks. In the course of time, the rectangular *sudaria* and *oraria* were folded lengthwise, like smaller versions of the *pallium*.

The vesture worn by liturgical ministers descended from these common articles of clothing of late antiquity. The white *(alba)* tunic, given to neophytes in baptism and worn as the common garment of ministers, became the alb. The amice *(amictum)* continued over time to be used just as it was in antiquity — to clothe the neck. The dalmatic became the distinctive liturgical garb of deacons. The *planeta* became the distinctive garb of priests and bishops under its other name of *casula* ("little house," since it enveloped the wearer), or chasuble.

The other garments mentioned — the *pallium, sudarium* and *orarium* — which were already reduced in size in antiquity to narrow bands, became ornaments. The *pallium* became a badge of distinction for imperial dignitaries; its use was extended to archbishops after the Edict of Toleration (313). The *sudarium* and the *orarium* gave us, respectively, the stole worn by bishops and priests and the stole worn by deacons. (Some historians, however, have argued that the stole is more directly descended from the Jewish prayer shawl.)

MEDIEVAL DEVELOPMENTS

Early medieval writers, reflecting on the rituals of the Jerusalem Temple, began to attribute symbolic meaning to each of the ministerial vestments.

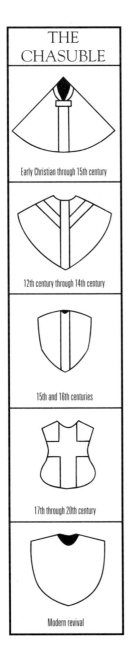

THE CHASUBLE

Early Christian through 15th century

12th century through 14th century

15th and 16th centuries

17th through 20th century

Modern revival

According to these writers, the alb signified purity of heart; the dalmatic, largesse; the chasuble, charity; the stoles, obedience — the yoke of Christ. It is noteworthy that what seems to impress these writers is the amplitude of the vesture. Works of art of the period reveal albs that were full and ample; dalmatics that reached nearly to the ankles, with full bodies and wide sleeves; chasubles that were cones of fabric that fell to the ankles, covering and enveloping the wearer and gathered up gracefully over the arms. They represented the virtues they signified at least in part by their amplitude.

For the ancients as well as for medieval people, God is distinguished by a generosity that is liberal to the point of "wasteful": the cup so full that it spills over, the measure that is packed down, shaken, and still overflows. God's generosity, echoed in the dedication of God's servants, is symbolized in the amplitude of their liturgical vesture. This generosity is an eschatological sign of what is to come. It is a sign of the sacred play and leisure of the reign of heaven.

Thus, by the medieval period, the principal elements of vesture were the alb, the dalmatic and the chasuble, garments that signify and clothe ministries — the baptized, the deacon, the priest and bishop.

The stoles (and the pallium) are marks of distinction, badges of office and authority. They are ornaments to the garments and are therefore secondary. The garments are the principal signs.

DEVOLUTION AND DECORATION

Over the centuries the dalmatic, which shrunk from ankle- to knee-length, was preserved even though the diaconate itself was reduced to a stage before presbyteral ordination. The chasuble shrunk much more dramatically from its full "conical" form. This was partly in response to the more intricate movements required of the priest by the increasingly elaborate liturgy. Material was first cut from the sides of the garment, giving us the so-called "Gothic" chasuble. In the sixteenth century, the chasuble was cut down even further — to shoulder width, and it was cut from heavy, stiffened fabric that hung down front and back to the knees — the Tridentine, or "fiddle-back" chasuble. Minimalism of form became rampant in the design and fabrication of vesture — epitomized by "stoles" the size of ribbons that priests carried in their pockets for emergencies.

Eventually, chasubles were decorated with orphreys, bands of brocade or embroidered cloth that covered the seam running down the front. From this practice, two principal forms developed: the cruciform-shaped and pallium-shaped orphreys. Dalmatics were decorated with two bands (claves) running down front and back at shoulder width. In antiquity, disciples honored their masters by venerating small images of them (an origin of the cult of icons); sometimes images were worn on clothing. Christians followed the custom as well, using one of the monograms of Christ (the *chi rho*, or a cross) or an image ("portrait") on the vesture. Sometimes, too, figures or symbols were woven into brocades, damasks and tapestries. Medieval vestments often were lavish in their use of embroidery.

LITURGICAL COLORS

There was little discussion of liturgical colors before the thirteenth century. It seems there was a general principle that called for the use of white for feasts and darker colors for mourning and for penitential seasons. In many places, the finest vestments, no matter what color, probably were used for feasts.

In his *De sacro altaris mysterio* (65), Lothar of Segni (1160–1216, Pope Innocent III from 1198) designates four liturgical colors — white, red, green and black — and their appropriate use throughout the year. These colors probably indicate Roman usage, or more specifically, that of the Roman Curia. Thus, for example, he says that while some use red for the feast of All Saints, white is more appropriate "as is done in the Roman Curia," because in the vision of John (Revelation 7:9), the elect from many nations stand before the throne in white robes. Similarly, he notes that red vestments may be worn for the feast of the Triumph of the Cross (September 14) because of the Passion, but he suggests that white vestments are preferable because the feast commemorates the discovery of the True Cross.

Lothar's scheme of colors for the church year is essentially the one we know today, except that he suggests black for mourning and times of abstinence, indicating the use of purple as an alternative. Following the medieval view that the literal meaning of scripture is the basis of a spiritual meaning that refers to the life of the church, Lothar deduces the meaning of the colors from scripture. He cites Song of Songs 5:10, where the Bride says of her Beloved, "He is all radiant and ruddy"; thus the church wears white on the feasts of virgins and confessors, and red on the feasts of apostles and martyrs. Black is worn for mourning and for times of abstinence, according to Lothar, because Song of Songs 1:5 says, "I am black, but beautiful, O daughters of Jerusalem." Green, according to Lothar, is "halfway between black and white," but he goes on to cite Song of Songs 4:13, which compares the Bride to an enclosed garden.

Such an understanding of color symbolism is not universal, however. White is not universally a color of joy and celebration, nor is black universally a color of mourning. Even within Western culture there is variety. For example, in Byzantine and medieval Western art, the Virgin is usually depicted in black or deep blue, which symbolizes the night sky from which rises

---

Here is an excerpt from the 1944 *Book of Ceremonies,* written by Laurence J. O'Connell, a priest of the archdiocese of Chicago and former master of ceremonies at Chicago's St. Mary of the Lake Seminary, Mundelein. The Latin vesting prayers come from the Roman Missal, and the contemporary English translations, not included in O'Connell's book, are provided by Martin Connell.

VESTING

Then, with the assistance of the server, put on the vestments in the following order.

1. The Amice: Take the amice at the two upper corners, kiss the cross, and bring the amice around to your back by swinging your right arm over your head. Rest the upper edge on your head for a moment and then place the amice on your shoulders. Cross the strings in front of you (right over left) and, bringing them around your body under your arms, tie them in front. Tuck the upper edge of the amice neatly inside your collar, placing the right side over the left in front. Recite the prayer:

Impone, Domine, capiti meo galeam salutis, ad expugnandos diabolicos incursus.

Put the helmet of salvation on my head, Lord, to fend off evil attacks.

2. The Alb: Take the alb with both hands. First put your head through, then your right arm, and then your left. Say the prayer:

Dealba me, Domine, et munda cor meum; ut, in Sanguine Agni dealbatus, gaudiis perfruar sempiternis.

Wash me, Lord, and cleanse my heart, so that, washed clean in the Blood of the Lamb, I may live in everlasting joy.

3. The Cincture: Take the cincture, folded double, with the tasseled ends to the right. Pass it around your waist and tie it in front with the tasseled ends almost touching the floor. Neatly arrange the alb to hang evenly all around, with no unsightly bunching in any one place. The prayer to be said while putting on the cincture is:

Praecinge me, Domine, cingulo puritatis, et exstingue in lumbis meis humorem libidinis; ut maneat in me virtus continentiae et castitatis.

the "sun of Justice." Thus in some medieval cultures, dark blue or black was used for feasts of the Virgin. Even within the context of European culture, then, a color can have more than one "meaning."

Color involves emotional and psychological factors, as we know from studies done on the effects that various colors have on people in their homes and workplaces, in advertising and so on. Colors and shades of colors can be soothing, arousing or neutral. The use of color in liturgical vesture (as well as in banners, paraments and other church textiles) should follow general color theory, be mindful of the tradition and be appropriate for the intended space.

CONTEMPORARY DESIGN

The liturgical movement of the nineteenth and early twentieth centuries sought to recover the authentic shape of ancient and medieval vestments. Through its efforts, the "fiddle-back" chasuble fell into disuse in most places prior to the Second Vatican

---

Wrap me round with the belt of purity, Lord, and extinguish all inclinations to evil, that a habit of self-control and fidelity may remain in me.

4. The Maniple: Take the maniple in your right hand, kiss the cross, and place it on your left arm, rather far back so that it will not interfere with your movements. Meanwhile, recite the prayer:

Merear, Domine, portare manipulum fletus et doloris; ut cum exsultatione recipiam mercedem laboris.

May I deserve to wear this cloth of weeping and lamentation, Lord, that I may receive to receive the reward of work.

5. The Stole: Take the stole in both hands. Kiss the cross and place the stole over your head so that it falls evenly on either side in front of you. Cross the two halves of the stole so that they form a cross in front, with the right half over the left; secure the ends of the stole by looping the ends of the cincture over them. Say:

Redde mihi, Domine, stolam immortalitatis, quam perdidi in praevaricatione primi parentis: et, quamvis indignus accedo ad tuum sacrum mysterium, merear tamen gaudium sempiternum.

Give back to me, Lord, the stole of immortality, which I lost in the lie of Adam and Eve, and, however unworthy I approach your holy mystery, may I nevertheless earn everlasting joy.

6. The Chasuble: While you are putting on the chasuble and tying the ribbons, say:

Domine, qui dixisti: Jugum meum suave est et onus meum leve: fac, ut istud portare sic valeam, quod consequar tuam gratiam. Amen.

You have said, Lord, that your yoke is easy and your burden is light. Grant that I may seek your grace and so be strong enough to wear this garment. Amen.

Council. But the leaders of the liturgical movement also allied themselves with those who sought to protect and preserve the traditional handicrafts and decorative arts in the face of increasing mass production. Manuals of liturgical arts and vestment-making appeared, as well as diatribes against mass-produced religious goods.

The *General Instruction of the Roman Missal* (306) says: "The beauty of a vestment should derive from its material and design rather than from lavish ornamentation. Representations on vestments should consist only of symbols, images or pictures portraying the sacred." In its brief section on liturgical vesture, *Environment and Art in Catholic Worship* (94) goes further than the *General Instruction of the Roman Missal*, saying: "The more these vestments fulfill their function by their color, design and enveloping form, the less they will need the signs, slogans and symbols which an unkind history has fastened on them." Although history, even ancient history, supports the use of symbols and images on vestments, we should reflect that originally vestments were not distinguished by their form or color from the apparel worn by the assembly. Once these "ordinary" garments became "distinctive" vesture for ritual worship, they themselves became symbolic. No other symbols were needed to set them apart. Moreover, a great deal of the symbolism applied to vestments is ill-conceived and superficial.

In my own work I have tried to fulfill the documents' prescriptions by creating truly enveloping forms, using the finest natural materials (wool and silk) and employing rich, bold colors. Further, I always try to make vesture that belongs to the place in which it will be used, and I try to use design and color to create visual continuity between seasons. Examples of this are the Advent and Christmas vesture designed for St. James Episcopal Cathedral in Chicago, and the Lenten and Easter vestments designed for St. Francis Xavier Church in St. Louis.

The Advent and Christmas chasubles for St. James Cathedral are both of the same design, having identical cruciform orphreys with a fleur-de-lis emblem and the same color lining — a deep, rich teal. The colors chosen suggest the theme of light dawning, which figures prominently in the seasons of Advent and Christmas. The outer layer of the Advent vestment is midnight blue; the orphreys are silver-gray and burgundy — the colors of the time just before dawn. The outer layer of the Christmas vestment for feasts of the Virgin will visually underscore the theological insight that we primarily celebrate the Virgin as Mother of God.

The design of the chasubles for St. Francis Xavier Church in St. Louis were inspired by the vesture worn by the angels in a stained-glass window (see page 31).

Photos: Ronald Zawilla

The Lenten vestment for St. Francis Xavier Church is made of a burgundy iridescent silk (red threads run vertically, blue threads horizontally). With the play of light caused by movement, the vestment shimmers richly. It is lined in red, signifying the theme of the Passion that slowly builds during Lent. The vestments used for Holy Week and the Triduum are lined in iridescent gold silk to signify the unity of the paschal mystery. The red and white vestment has the colors of Lent with the addition of green (the complement of red, making the red even brighter). The Easter vestment is of similar design, but the somber colors of the red vestment's orphrey are replaced with bright red, gold, turquoise and magenta. It is used only for Easter and for solemnities of the Lord during the year.

With the St. James vesture, the "movement" of colors from blues, silver and burgundy to white, blue and gold within a unifying form was meant to suggest the dawning of light in the night sky. It is a painterly, if abstract, way of commenting on one of the themes of Advent and Christmas.

The vestments for St. Francis Xavier Church attempt the same use of color. The utter simplicity yet richness of the Lenten vestment is meant to evoke the spirit of penance, imitating the suffering of Christ. The common form of the paschal vestments with their gold linings reminds us that the distinct events we commemorate on Palm Sunday, Good Friday, Easter and Pentecost are moments of a single movement, the exaltation of the Lord Jesus. In both parishes, the traditional lines of the architectural setting suggested to me more traditional lines for the vesture; a contemporary setting might evoke different styles.

Assuredly, people do notice vesture, and the celebration is enhanced by the use of distinctive, beautiful vesture. When vesture has been designed for a particular place through the choice

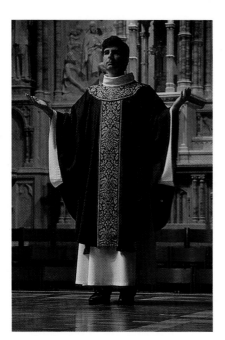

The violet chasuble for St. Francis Xavier Church.
Photo: Ronald Zawilla

of colors and forms that are "at home" there, they cease to be merely "what the priest is wearing" and belong to the place and to the assembly. The carrying over of the colors of one season into the next and the repetition of decorative motifs remind us of the underlying unity of events.

Given the history of vesture, I favor the use of a stole worn under the chasuble. It is neater, the chasuble usually hangs better, and the presider is less likely to fuss with the stole. In addition, wearing the stole on the outside duplicates symbol: Both chasuble and stole indicate priestly ministry. Stoles worn on the outside also seem to be voids that people love to fill with symbols and even words; or, because people feel that the stole needs to contrast the chasuble, upholstery or drapery fabrics in plaids and stripes are chosen. Such fancy stoles may only be necessary when worn over an alb without a chasuble or dalmatic for rites such as blessings.

Angels in a window at
St. Francis Xavier Church
inspired the vesture for
the church's ministers.
Photo: Ronald Zawilla

THINGS TO LOOK FOR IN VESTURE

Lined chasubles and dalmatics can be exquisite; a richly contrasting color can be used for the lining. Using the same kind of
fabric for the lining as the outer layer assures proper draping and

The red chasuble for St. Francis Xavier Church.
Note the contrasting color of the lining.

Photo: Ronald Zawilla

avoids bunching. A cheap lining is no bargain; it will wear out before the outer fabric does. Silk is light enough to be lined and still be comfortable. If a vestment is unlined, the hems and seams ought to lay flat with no puckering.

There is nothing inherently wrong with synthetics, but they tend to be heavier and warmer than natural fabrics. Natural fibers do need some care: a good dry cleaning, perhaps an occasional steaming. But if cared for properly, natural fibers will look better longer than synthetic fibers will.

Let figures and images appear on banners or other sacred art. The chasuble is not a backdrop for pictures or a bulletin board for slogans. Overusing a symbol weakens its ability to speak. I remember an ordination where the bishop's vesture included an overlay stole covered with large, bold crosses; the matching miter had the same decoration, and he was wearing a pectoral cross outside of the chasuble — ten crosses in all. Had he been an archbishop, he would also have been wearing the pallium with its several crosses. The multiplicity of crosses marred the vesture and rendered the cross a visual cliché. The liturgy and its assembly is much better served by ample, graceful, colorful vesture that evokes through form and texture and color a deep respect for the great mysteries that we celebrate.

White, raw silk, conical style chasuble and stole by Vincent de Paul Crosby. Note the graceful draping of this style of chasuble. Photo: Vincent de Paul Crosby

CONICAL CHASUBLE BY VINCENT DE PAUL CROSBY

◦ ◦ ◦

Vesting the book

This festive lectionary cover of raw silk appliqués on linen attests to the dignity of the scriptures while preserving the book.

Photo: Vincent de Paul Crosby

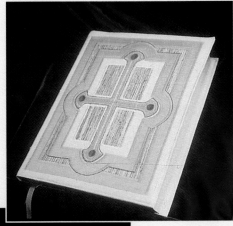

◦ ◦ ◦

Vesting the head

Natural Tussah silk mitre with traditional Kente cloth banding.

Photo: Vincent de Paul Crosby

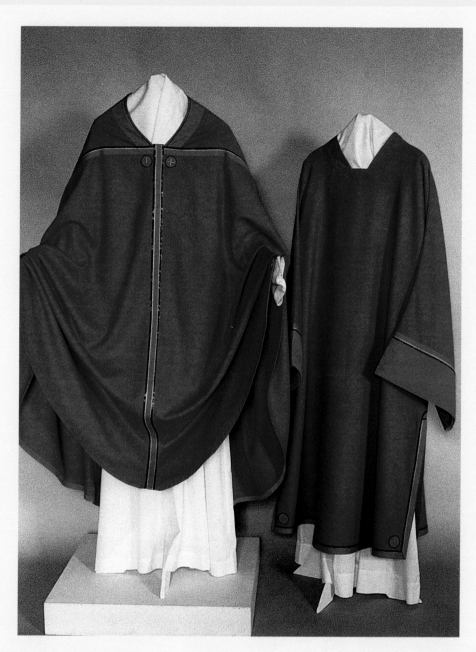

Worsted wool chasuble (left) and dalmatic (right). The dalmatic was introduced in the West as an outer garment for deacons around the year 190, at which time it was considered rather "secular."

Photo: Vincent de Paul Crosby

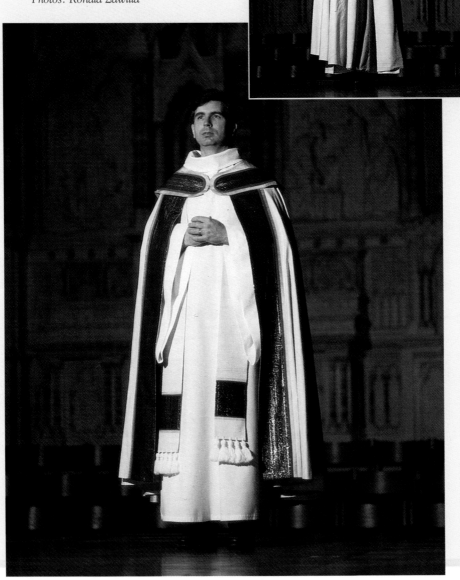

The cope is a festive outer vestment that lends dignity to a variety of rites. It is not restricted to the ordained; it also may be worn by a cantor singing the Exsultet or by a layperson presiding at vespers. The cope, stole and alb pictured here were created by Ronald Zawilla.

Photos: Ronald Zawilla

◦− COPE BY RONALD ZAWILLA −◦

36

THE COPE

Ronald John Zawilla

Previous chapters have discussed the alb, the vestment of the baptized, and the stole, dalmatic and chasuble, the additional vesture for ordained ministers. This chapter will examine a vestment for ministers — most often the presider — that is not widely used now but should be reconsidered: the cope.

Prior to Vatican II, the cope was worn for processions and especially for celebrations of benediction of the blessed sacrament. The recent decline of such devotions and a growing neominimalism have all but eliminated the use of the cope. A chasuble and stole are standard for Mass, at least on Sundays. A stole worn over an alb is commonly all that is used for other celebrations, sometimes even for daily Mass. The one time a cope might be used today is for the solemn transfer of the eucharist on Holy Thursday, but even then some presiders simply don a humeral veil over the chasuble.

This is unfortunate because the cope is a graceful, beautiful vestment that can lend dignity to a celebration: the service of light at the Easter Vigil, baptism or marriage outside of Mass, or daily prayer, for example. And unlike the chasuble and the dalmatic, the cope can be worn over an alb by anyone who is baptized, depending on his or her ministry in a given celebration. It is not restricted to the ordained, so the cantor singing the *Exsultet* may wear a cope, or the nonordained presider at vespers may wear one.

HISTORY OF USE

The ancestors of the cope are the same as those of the chasuble:
the ancient Roman outer garments known as the *paenula* and
the *casula*. Both these outer garments were made from semicircular pieces of cloth. Sometimes the straight edges were sewn
together, forming the cone-like garments that became the chasuble of Christian use. Sometimes the straight edges were left
open and the edges were joined at the neck with a brooch or
with ties. In this latter form, the garment often had a hood. It
was made of heavy wool or felt to protect the wearer from rain
or winter cold and was called a *pluviale* ("raincoat"). These heavy
overcoats originated among the poor, who probably also used
them as blankets on cold nights. Eventually the military adopted
these cloaks, and then the upper class.

The journey from common apparel to liturgical vesture followed two routes. First, monks, canons and friars, as well as parish priests, wore cloaks of rough, heavy wool as overcoats. They
were even worn indoors during the winter in northern Europe,
where the great cathedrals and churches were — and in many
cases still are — unheated. In this way the *cappa(-ae)* became
part of the religious habit, especially for the mendicant orders
such as the Dominicans and Carmelites. The *cappa* became choir
dress. Dominicans, for example, wore the *cappa* in choir from
the feast of the Exaltation of the Cross (September 14) until the
Easter Vigil, when it was removed with great flourish during the
singing of the Gloria.

Meanwhile, in a second route of design development, people
of the upper classes began to wear the *cappa*, making theirs of
more luxurious fabrics such as silk and embellishing the straight
edges with embroidery and appliqué work. The brooches used to
secure the *cappa* were often made of precious metals set with
gems. Bishops, as officials of the Roman Empire, were entitled
to wear these garments of the nobility. The *cappa* became a court
garment worn for ceremonial occasions. Sumptuously decorated
cappae were often given as diplomatic gifts in the early Middle
Ages. Cardinals, bishops, priests and canons, like monks and friars, wore the *cappa* in church for added warmth, and thus it
became choir dress for them as well.

Sometimes the *cappa* was made in such a way that the lower
part trailed on the ground, forming a train. The length of the
train was a mark of the dignity of the wearer: Remember the
twelve-foot *cappae magnae* of the cardinals that were shortened
by Pope Paul VI? The medieval canons — diocesan clergy living in community — often wore luxurious *cappae* lined with fur,

as can be seen in many brass tomb-rubbings from European churches. This extravagance sometimes elicited censure from medieval councils and synods.

The cope originated, then, first as a utilitarian garment, becoming in time ritual dress. Accordingly, medieval commentaries on the liturgy, which usually have a section on the vestments and their mystical significance, do not mention the cope. Gradually, however, the cope became a liturgical vestment for use by presiders at the liturgical hours, in processions and for celebration of sacraments other than eucharist. On festive occasions, ministers other than subdeacons, deacons, priests and bishops — all of whom had their own distinct vesture — might be outfitted in copes.

HISTORY OF DESIGN

The cope traditionally has been made from a semicircle of cloth. Frequently, the straight edge of the semicircle was decorated with a band of rich fabric, often metallic, and embroidered. A rectangular piece of cloth, called a morse, was used to join the edges of the cope at the neck. Sometimes a semicircular opening was cut for the neck and tucks were sewn in at the shoulders to help the cope sit more comfortably and securely on the shoulders. Most copes had hoods. In time, the hood, which was originally utilitarian, became vestigial. It might be a real hood reduced in size or a large, flat collar covering the shoulders and upper back of the wearer.

The decoration of copes parallels the decoration of chasubles. It was the straight edge of the cope and the morse that were usually embellished. But in the Middle Ages, sometimes the entire surface of the cope was lavishly embroidered with images and laden with gems. In the Baroque period, copes, like chasubles, were often made of heavy, stiff material. The collars became somewhat like banners affixed to the lower edge of the decorative border, which means that they hung artificially low on the back. These large panels, which had lost any resemblance whatever to a real hood, were often heavily encrusted with decoration. I remember attending in my youth a celebration of benediction at which the presider was attired in one of these heavy copes. When he genuflected, he disappeared behind the heavy material, which did not move with him.

CONTEMPORARY DESIGN

I think that copes should be made of medium-weight wool or silk: They should hang in beautiful folds and move easily with the presider, adding grace to gestures and movement. Lining a cope provides the opportunity to use contrasting color; adding a decorative border to the straight edges helps the cope hang well. I usually make copes with large, round collars that rest easily on the shoulders and give the garment extra stability at the neck. Hoods seem to be superfluous, since they would never be used. As with chasubles, copes should not be billboards for unnecessary images or symbols. The beauty of the materials, the cut of the garment and the quality of the sewing should speak for themselves. (See, for example, the photos on page 36.)

USING THE COPE

Depending on the nature of the assembly and the degree of the solemnity of the occasion, the cope may be used at Mass. On Holy Thursday, the cope may be worn for the transfer of the eucharist, and at the Vigil from the lighting of the fire through the liturgy of baptism. Although the flow of the liturgy should not be broken by the presider's "costume change," to wear the cope on the Sundays of Easter for the entrance procession and sprinkling rite surely would be a way of expressing the joyous festivity and solemnity of the season. Likewise, on great solemnities when the altar is to be incensed at the beginning of Mass, the cope would be appropriate. In such cases, the change to chasuble can be accomplished unobtrusively either after the opening prayer, while people are getting settled and the lector is approaching the ambo, or perhaps at the preparation of the gifts. (At the Vigil, especially when baptism is done by immersion, the presider can remove the cope before entering the font and don the chasuble when he goes off to put on dry clothes.)

The use of the cope by the presider would lend dignity and solemnity to celebrations that occur outside of Mass: baptism, particularly during the Easter season; weddings; communal celebrations of reconciliation; wake services; vigil services; morning and evening prayer; benediction, stations of the cross and other devotions.

THE USE OF LITURGICAL COLORS

G. Thomas Ryan

For the first millennium, little attention was paid to creating fixed cycles of colors for the vestments that were related to particular seasons and feasts, though white was always central. Through the Middle Ages, most dioceses and local communities of Western and Central Europe began developing and sharing customs that associated certain days with certain colors. Until 1570, when Roman authorities issued universal rules as part of the Tridentine reforms, these patterns differed from region to region and from parish to parish.

This system, now 400 years old, has been accepted by each successive generation and was repeated in the recent reforms. It has been an enduring and popular part of the Tridentine heritage because Western Christians see it as assisting their progress through the liturgical year, as lending a seasonal unity and as expressing the shifting moods of the assembly.

But there are at least two ways of thinking about these colors that are decidedly unhelpful. The first is to think of the colors as mere decorations, as mobile parts of the environment. Sure, the colors and shapes add to the experience, but ministers should never be treated as props, as part of a "matched set" in a pretty diorama. The second unhelpful way of thinking about colors is to see them as carrying allegorical or mystical meanings. Their value is in providing seasonal contrast and mood, not in imparting didactic messages.

The list of vestment colors for Masses and for all other liturgies is found in the *General Instruction of the Roman Missal* (308–310).

White:

- festive seasons of Christmas and Easter
- days of the Lord — except days related to the passion
- days of saints — except the anniversary of death of martyrs, apostles, evangelists
- Conversion of Paul, Chair of Peter, Birth of John the Baptist, All Saints, John the Evangelist — days associated with martyrs or apostles, but not anniversaries of martyrdom

Red:

- Passion/Palm Sunday and Good Friday
- Pentecost
- days of the Lord related to the passion
- days of martyrs, apostles, evangelists

(If only a few red vestments are owned by a community, they should not be so specifically decorated for the Passion, for Pentecost, or for martyrs that they cannot be used on all these days.)

Green:

- Ordinary Time

Violet:

- Advent
- Lent

(If only a few violet vestments are available, Lenten and penitential motifs should not be so prevalent as to disallow their use in Advent.)

Rose:

- The Third Sunday of Advent
- The Fourth Sunday of Lent

(When there are limited resources, this old tradition need not be kept, and violet can be worn.)

Gold or more precious colors and materials:

- solemn occasions

Funerals and liturgies on November 2 can utilize white, violet and even black vesture. The Tridentine rule was black — a very dramatic choice — but many reformers in the 1960s felt that eternal life would be better expressed by white vesture. Others countered that this was too festive and joyous, insensitive to the real mourning and pain. Still others suggested a middle ground: the darker color of violet.

Each community should review its policy on choosing vesture for funerals. In the context of existing pastoral practice and other decorations, a case might be made for one color over another. Perhaps the seasons and colors already in the church complex should be respected. Violet could be used at funerals through Advent and Lent, white during the weeks of Christmas and Easter, black during Ordinary Time. If the community has a truly worthy chasuble in any one of these colors, then this might be the best choice. The chasuble does not need to match the casket pall.

There is no need to memorize any of these lists, to worry about whether to give priority to a season's color or to the color of a particular day. The annual ordo in every sacristy lists the correct color for each day. When optional memorials are selected for a given parish, they determine the color for the day; these, too, are in the ordo. When votive or other special Masses are celebrated, their colors are of the given day (unless there is an obvious association, like red with Masses of the Holy Spirit). As we become ever more aware of our local resources, of the emotional power of varied colors and of visual relationships, we can breath fresh life into this enduring system of linking seasons and affections.

THE VESTMENTS OF KATREEN BETTENCOURT

THE ARTIST'S STATEMENT

Because the assembly gathers in the presence of God to cele-brate his saving deeds . . . it cannot be satisfied with anything less than the beautiful in its environment and in all its artifacts. . . . Admittedly difficult to define, the beautiful is related . . . to the holy. . . .

Environment and Art in Catholic Worship, 34

Thomas Aquinas says, "Three things are needed for beauty: wholeness, harmony and radiance." For vesture for the liturgy, these translate into integrity, quality and rapture.

Integrity: Vesture has to be an honest expression of the artisan. Vesture for the liturgy requires integrity of its raw materials, too. The closer its components are to nature, the more integral that created thing will be.

Quality: That the things we use in worship must be of high quality does not need explanation or justification.

Rapture: Yes, rapture! Ritual objects should be fascinating, should sow the seeds of ecstasy. Once you are enraptured by something, you are taken inside of it. It ceases to exist merely outside of you, and therefore it ceases to be able to distract you. Vesture should activate that initial attraction to the beholder, but then once it has captured the beholder by its beauty become part of the ritual action and thus be one more stepping stone to the contemplation of Divine Beauty. Fads and frills will not do!

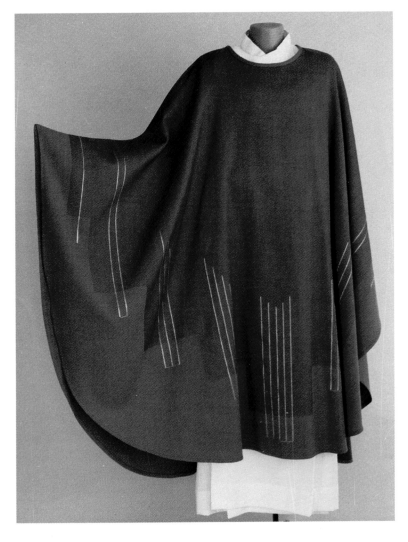

Katreen Bettencourt's Gothic style chasuble is woven of purple silk and rose wool on a cotton warp. It can be worn reversed from purple to rose, on Gaudete Sunday, for example.

Photo: Katreen Bettencourt

Since vesture is made of fabric, which flows and drapes, its designs ought not be static (as, say, in a painting), but should be alive, like the cloth itself. The designs should have an element of surprise, of wonder, of mystery that unfolds with each movement. A good design will have details that can be detected and appreciated only close up, when one approaches for communion, or in the course of a procession. A good design will display both bold and subtle elements — achieved mostly through the use of color.

Because vesture is for people, it is a ritual focal point. But the ultimate effectiveness of the vestment depends on the one wearing it. It is only when the presider or other minister can bear the garment with dignity, grace and serenity that the vesture will have its full effect.

This square-cut chasuble was woven with blue and red-purple silks and teal wool on a cotton warp. This weave is polychrome, using the weft yarns constantly to allow for more color variation. While blue is not a Roman liturgical color, it is used by some Lutherans in Advent. Photo: Katreen Bettencourt

This Gothic-style chasuble was woven with green silk and purple wool on a cotton warp. It is reversible from green to purple.
Photo: Katreen Bettencourt

Of this conical-style chasuble in white silk and black wool on a cotton warp, Katreen writes, "Death leads to resurrection, but those who stay behind are still fully human, and sorrow is part of the human condition. While most churches in the United States use white for funerals, here I wanted to incorporate the rich color black. White silk woven with black cotton becomes a rich silver platinum. The streaks of burgundy, salmon and pink add surprise."
Photo: Katreen Bettencourt

This festive cope is of white silk and gold-colored wool on a cotton warp. It is one piece of fabric, without any seam.

Photo: Katreen Bettencourt

THE VESTMENTS OF VINCENT DE PAUL CROSBY

THE ARTIST'S STATEMENT

Clothing is symbolic. Its use, be it a fig leaf or a fur coat, is common to all humanity, and it does more than simply protect one from the elements. It says something about who the person is and the role that the person plays in society. Clothing has a history, and those vested in it bear the traditions of their people.

Scripture speaks of God as "clothed in majesty and glory, wrapped in light as in a robe." From swaddling clothes to holy shroud, Jesus is clothed in this glory. And since in baptism Christians are said to have "put on Christ," we, too, are vested: no longer to cover our shame but to reveal our glory as children of God and heirs of heaven in Christ Jesus.

We use vestments in the liturgy not just to fulfill ritual requirements but to reveal meaning, to capture imagination and to point to the mystery of faith. So we can never be satisfied — and the liturgy is never served — with vesture of poor design and cut, didactic and superficial symbolism, and a general lack of quality that renders it incapable of bearing mystery.

49

In ritual celebrations of those made holy in baptism, even the objects used become holy and are treated with reverence. We not only vest people, but we also dress the altar, drape the cross, cover books and veil vessels. This is no mere exercise in ecclesial interior decorating; rather, it is an essential embodiment of faith.

I prefer to have personal contact with each client. I enter into a "design dialogue" with the client to determine specific needs and to understand the place and space in which the vesture will be used. If I can, I visit the place. If I can't, I ask for pictures. With this information, I prepare sketches that are submitted in the form of a proposal, indicating cost and including fabric samples. When this is approved, the proposal is signed, a down payment made, and work proceeds according to an agreed upon schedule.

Throughout history, the Benedictine monastic family has shared the gifts of its monks and nuns with the whole church. Benedict himself wrote: "Artisans present in the monastery should practice their crafts with humility, as permitted by the abbot." In the very first years of its foundation over 150 years ago, St. Vincent Archabbey was reminded of this fact when our founder, Boniface Wimmer, wrote: "Art must go hand in hand with religion . . . it is the duty of monasteries to foster, to promote, and to spread art, especially religious art."

Detail of the rich design of a g
chasuble (see at right) by Vin
de Paul Crosby.
Photo: Vincent de Paul Crosby

50

Conical chasuble and stole for Ordinary Time; the foundation cloth is iridescent green silk brocade. The fullness of a conical chasuble requires deliberateness of gesture on the part of the one wearing it.

Photo: Vincent de Paul Crosby

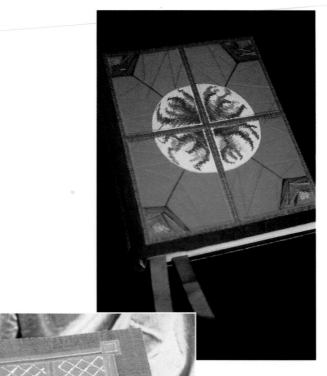

Lectionary cover for
Ordinary Time. The leaf motif
(silk appliqués) suggests
growth in the life of faith.

Photo: Vincent de Paul Crosby

Lectionary cover for Lent.
Mixed fabrics appliquéd to a
linen foundation.

Photo: Vincent de Paul Crosby

For more of Vincent de Paul Crosby's vestments, see pages 33 – 35.

CLOTHED IN GLORY
THE ALTAR AND THE BUILDING

The LORD said to Moses: You shall make the tabernacle with ten curtains of fine twisted linen, and blue, purple, and crimson yarns; you shall make them with cherubim skillfully worked into them. The length of each curtain shall be twenty-eight cubits, and the width of each curtain four cubits; all the curtains shall be of the same size. Five curtains shall be joined to one another; and the other five curtains shall be joined to one another. You shall make loops of blue on the edge of the outermost curtain in the first set; and likewise you shall make loops on the edge of the outermost curtain in the second set. . . . You shall make fifty clasps of gold, and join the curtains to one another with the clasps, so that the tabernacle may be one whole.

You shall also make curtains of goats' hair for a tent over the tabernacle; you shall make eleven curtains. . . . You shall join five curtains by themselves, and six curtains by themselves, and the sixth curtain you shall double over at the front of the tent. You shall make fifty loops on the edge of the curtain that is outermost in one set, and fifty loops on the edge of the curtain that is outermost in the second set.

You shall make fifty clasps of bronze and put the clasps into the loops, and join the tent together, so that it may be one whole. . . . You shall make for the tent a covering of tanned rams' skins and an outer covering of fine leather.

Exodus 26:1–6, 7, 9–11, 14

Moses said to all the congregation of the Israelites: All who are skillful among you shall come and make all that the LORD has commanded: the tabernacle, its tent and its covering, its clasps and its frames, its bars, its pillars and its bases; the ark with its poles, the mercy seat, and the curtain for the screen.

Exodus 35:4, 10–12

And they came, everyone whose heart was stirred, and everyone whose spirit was willing, and brought the LORD's offering to be used for the tent of the meeting, and for its service, and for the sacred vestments. . . . And everyone who possessed blue or purple or crimson yarn or fine linen or goats' hair or tanned rams' skins or fine leather, brought them.

Exodus 35:21, 23

All the skillful women spun with their hands, and brought what they had spun in blue and purple and crimson yarns and fine linen; all the women whose hearts moved them to use their skill spun the goats' hair.

Exodus 35:25–26

Then Moses said to the Israelites: "See, the LORD has called by name Bezalel son of Uri son of Hur, of the tribe of Judah; he has filled him with divine spirit, with skill, intelligence and knowledge in every kind of craft, to devise artistic designs. . . . And he has inspired him to teach, both him and Oholiab son of Ahisamach, of the tribe of Dan. He has filled them with skill to do every kind of work done by an artisan or by a designer or by an embroiderer in blue, purple, and crimson yarns, and in fine linen, or by a weaver — by any sort of artisan or skilled designer.

Exodus 35:30–32, 34–35

All those with skill among the workers made the tabernacle with ten curtains; they were made of fine twisted linen, and blue, purple, and crimson yarns, with cherubim skillfully worked into them. The length of each curtain was twenty-eight cubits, and the width of each curtain four cubits; all the curtains were of the same size.

Exodus 36:8–9

Bezalel joined five curtains to one another, and the other five curtains he joined to one another. He made loops of blue on the edge of the outermost curtain of the first set; likewise he made them on the edge of the outermost curtain of the second set; he made fifty loops on the one curtain, and he made fifty loops on the edge of the curtain that was in the second set: the loops were opposite one another. And he made fifty clasps of gold, and joined the curtains one to the other with clasps so the tabernacle was one whole.

He also made curtains of goats' hair for a tent over the tabernacle; he made eleven curtains. . . . He joined five curtains by themselves, and six curtains by themselves. He made fifty loops on the edge of the outermost curtain of the one set, and fifty loops on the edge of the other connecting curtain. He made fifty clasps of bronze to join the tent together so that it might be one whole. And he made for the tent a covering of tanned rams' skins and an outer covering of fine leather.

Exodus 36:10–14, 16–19

Now when David settled in his house, David said to the prophet Nathan, "I am living in a house of cedar, but the ark of the covenant of the LORD is under a tent." Nathan said to David, "Do all that you have in mind, for God is with you."

But that same night, the word of the LORD came to Nathan, saying: Go and tell my servant David: Thus says the LORD: You shall not build me a house to live in. For I have not lived in a house since the day I brought out Israel to this very day, but I have lived in a tent and a tabernacle. . . . Moreover, I declare to you that the LORD shall build you a house.

1 Chronicles 17:1–5, 10

After building the Temple Solomon made the curtain of blue and purple and crimson fabrics and fine linen, and worked cherubim into it.

2 Chronicles 3:14

Then Jesus cried out again with a loud voice and breathed his last. At that moment the curtain of the Temple was torn in two, from top to bottom.

Matthew 27:50–51

Then Peter and the other disciple set out and went toward the tomb. The two were running together, but the other disciple outran Peter and reached the tomb first. He bent down to look in and saw the linen wrappings lying there, but he did not go in. Then Simon Peter came, following him, and went into the tomb. He saw the linen wrapping lying there, and the cloth that had been on Jesus' head, not lying with the linen wrappings but rolled up in a place by itself.

John 20:3 – 7

May we shout for joy over your victory,
and in the name of our God set up our banners.

Psalm 20:5

We have this hope, a sure and steadfast anchor of the soul, a hope that enters the inner shrine behind the curtain, where Jesus, a forerunner on our behalf, has entered, having become a high priest forever according to the order of Melchizedek.

Hebrews 6:19

Therefore, my friends, since we have confidence to enter the sanctuary by the blood of Jesus, by the new and living way that he opened for us through the curtain (that is, through his flesh), and since we have a great priest over the house of God, let us approach with a true heart in full assurance of faith, with our hearts sprinkled clean from an evil conscience and our bodies washed with pure water.

Hebrews 10:19

TEXTILES FOR THE CHURCH
A PRIMER

Connie Cassani Beard

This chapter is a general introduction to textiles for the church building. Banners are the standard forms, defined as movable, changeable artwork made by piecing, appliquéing, layering and embellishing cloth.

WHY BANNERS?

Textiles can be attractive, affordable ways to enrich the liturgy and its space. They can invite us to prayer and encourage our participation in the action. The variety of colors, textures and patterns available in fabrics offers great design flexibility; and a pool of labor in the form of amateur sewers is present in most parishes. The cost of banners varies greatly, depending on the quality of fabric used and the complexity of the design.

The problem with a banner usually comes in the design stage. The designer needs to know what is appropriate for a certain place on a certain occasion. The ease of making banners can lead to their gross misuse. Cranking out pieces to fill a space or meet a demand for seasonal decor can be detrimental to good design and good textile art. The tendency to make disposable banners with a life expectancy of only a year or two can result in pieces of poor quality that have no real value, even in the short run. Of all the arts and crafts employed for the church's worship, banners lead in the "schlock" category — inappropriate designs, cheap materials, poor execution, poor installation, and perhaps all done for the wrong reasons.

PROCESS

The process of banner-making involves more than choosing colors, materials, cutters and sewers. Designing can mean praying about and living with ideas and images, searching for insight into how to convey a message without words, and spending time in the space where the banner will be installed. Designers need to let their imaginations go beyond what may be understood as customary or traditional for the particular occasion or season. It is important to articulate clearly why a banner is desired — for what season, what feast, what need? The designer (who may very well be someone other than the commissioning persons, the cutters, sewers and installers) is responsible for visualizing how the banner can fill the specific need and for communicating this to others.

TYPES

Banners may hang freely in space, hang against a wall or hang on or over furniture (these are called paraments). Or they may be designed to be carried in procession. When free-hanging, banners can alter the feeling or definition of the space and even create new spaces; they can lend an appropriate atmosphere for a certain season or feast; and they can establish an otherwise non-existent focus or hide an undesirable focus (such as backlighting).

Wall-hanging banners do just that — hang on walls — which allows the appearance of the space to change but not its shape (figure 1). Paraments can be very effective in modifying the appearance of poorly designed or poorly fashioned altars and ambos or in providing a seasonal accent to liturgical furnishings in general.

Processional banners are associated with movement, but when stationary they also perform some of the same functions as the pieces mentioned above. Processional banners seem to work best when they are long and narrow.

DESIGN

"Among the symbols with which the liturgy deals, none is more important than the assembly of believers" (*Environment and Art in Catholic Worship*, 28). "If instead of serving and aiding the action [of the assembly], they [art images] threaten it or compete with it, then they are unsuitable" (EACW, 98) With such a great range of sizes and colors, design restraint is often needed to keep banners from dominating the space or action they are intended to serve. In my home parish (a 1920s processional-style worship space seating about 400), at Pentecost we decorated the entire nave by draping strips of red fabric (one on each side of the center aisle) in a looping fashion across the bottom of the roof trusses (about 20 feet above the floor). Where the assembly gathers to receive communion, we suspended three pieces of red fabric on each side of a triangular open canopy. The flowing, flame-symbol canopy seemed to complement the assembly's action without dominating it (figure 2).

Color selection should be appropriate for the liturgical season or feast, and it should harmonize with the light and colors in the space already. When in doubt, it's better to err on the side of subtlety. Carefully adding an accent color can create an element of surprise. For Advent, our altar (3' x 8') was draped with a predominantely blue cloth with a 12-inch purple border. Between the blue and purple there was one line of green piping, creating a small but pleasant surprise.

TECHNIQUES

Various methods of appliqué, piecing, quilting, layering and interweaving fabric strips and ribbons, as well as combinations of these methods, allow for tremendous design latitude. The use of embellishments such as beads, embroidery and ribbons can be particularly effective in strengthening the focal point as well as adding finishing touches.

Techniques need to be compatible with materials. Certain techniques are not appropriate with certain kinds of fabric. For example, pieces that combine lightweight and heavyweight fabrics often hang unevenly and out of balance; finely woven cloth is better suited to banners that are intended to be pieced or appliquéd or that will employ refined details.

FABRICS

It generally makes sense to choose fabrics that are locally available. A fabric's beauty lies in its color, texture and weave. Cotton, linen, rayon, silk (particularly raw silk), wool and blends of these provide a shelf of basic materials. For more texture and larger sizes, consider upholstery and drapery materials. Also consider the beautiful and rich brocades, satins, silks and velvets found in many old vestments and paraments. Pulling them out of the closet and using them as a resource to enliven new textiles for church use not only reflects a certain sense of stewardship and tradition but also extends the design possibilities. The best design and craft will be wasted if the materials employed are not of high quality.

THE ALTAR CLOTH AND OTHER LINENS

G. Thomas Ryan

In the rich variety of ritual circumstance and physical movement, many textiles have become convenient, even necessary,
for liturgical communities. Cloth is used not only to make clothes
and wall decoration, but it is also used to cover tables, clean vessels and absorb moisture. We use textiles, often linen, to cover
furniture, to cleanse vessels and to dry people after baptism.

LINEN

The plagues upon Egypt included the destruction of its flax by
hail (Exodus 9:31); flax was an important part of the country's
economy. From the stalks of their flax plants, the Egyptians fabricated the most highly prized linen of the ancient world. It was
traditionally specified for use in the temple at Jerusalem. It was
used to wrap the dead and to make clothing, bedsheets, curtains, sails for ships and wrappers for scrolls.

In Christian communities, linen was used for the first altar
covers. It was the premier fabric for public rites and for burial,
for vesting symbols of the body of Christ (altar and people). For
two millennia, Christian churches prescribed linen for a wide
variety of purposes. It was the fabric of choice for albs and altar
cloths as well as for the smaller textiles in the church.

The use of linen is no longer mandated, and other fabrics are
often used now, chiefly cotton or polyester blended with either
cotton or linen. Still, the beauty and functionality of linen continue to make it the ideal material for many of the smaller textile items discussed in this chapter. Pure linen may be more

expensive, but it probably functions better and lasts much longer than the alternatives. It is also true that it probably wrinkles more readily, but most of these items should be laundered and pressed after every use anyway. Whatever material is chosen, it should launder well. Bear in mind that white fabric without polyester probably will come out cleanest after laundering, because higher water temperatures can be used. Whenever it comes time to order new textiles, always evaluate all the available fabrics with an eye to their past performance.

As were the vestments, so too corporals, purificators, palls, veils, gremials and towels were often decorated with symbols that duplicated and trivialized the larger and stronger symbols in the place for worship. (Red crosses were either stitched or embroidered onto the smaller linens.) Added symbols and decoration are never necessary and are usually distracting. This holds especially true for older items that have been decorated with strips of lace. No matter how praiseworthy or traditional the use of lace may be in certain domestic items such as draperies, its use in liturgy is too frivolous, too linked to this kind of secular ornamentation.

ORIGINS OF THE ALTAR CLOTH

The earliest Christians lived in a region where fine linen, especially linen from Egypt, had been highly prized for centuries. Ritual laws, codified in the book of Exodus, often demanded the use of this Egyptian cloth for screens, tabernacle hangings and vestments. This same linen or similar fabrics made from flax were used for burial shrouds. It is no surprise, then, that primitive documents from the Mediterranean basin make note of the use of one fine linen cover for the altar — carrying rich memories of burial shrouds and of vesture for the most significant public rites. It was placed on the altar at the start of the eucharistic rite and removed at its end.

LATER USAGE

It seems that by the year 1000, communities preferred to leave this cloth on the altar at all times. Local customs for such cloths continued to evolve, often multiplying their number on the altar. Eventually, communities allied with the Roman rite followed the same code, using three linen (or hemp) cloths on the altar. Some communities took to dying their cloths various colors, but white was virtually universal. Because the altars had almost always been moved to the wall or had retablos reared up behind them, cloths never covered the rear of the altar. For the front of the altar, communities went to great lengths to procure lavish frontals (antependia), often of the color of the liturgical season.

Many sacristies still have cloths from old altars. These typically include white linen top cloths ("fair linens," long enough to hang to the floor on each end); two linen undercloths for each altar (or wider cloths that, when folded, yield two layers); and a chrismale (or "cerecloth," linen waxed on one side and of the exact dimensions of each altar's surface). This last was the cloth that was placed under the other three at the dedication rite and could be used permanently. In addition, there were cloths for placement over all the other cloths when candelabra were used and for each altar a "vesperale," or dust cover, that was placed over the other cloths between services.

CURRENT NORMS

The regulations have been radically reduced to a single norm (*General Instruction of the Roman Missal*, 268):

> At least one cloth should be placed on the altar out of reverence for the celebration of the memorial of the Lord and the banquet that gives us his body and blood. The shape, size and decoration of the altar cloth should be in keeping with the design of the altar.

Though the directive is general, its application is to be very specific, for each and every cover should be fabricated with a specific altar in mind. A cover designed for a wall-mounted altar should not be used on a free-standing altar. Such a cloth will cover only the top and sides, looking like large scarf.

Two patterns are rightly favored at this point in the reforms. Often the cloth is of the exact dimensions of the table top. In other places, the cloth will be longer, even to the extent that it might go to the floor on all four sides. This fullest form, termed "Laudean" or "Jacobean" (perhaps related to their usage in England at the time of King James), can create an appearance of great dignity while also serving to conceal a poorly made altar. On the negative side, it will also conceal a well-made altar and perhaps diminish the community's sense of the altar as a form.

Some communities with strong, well-made altars have been rediscovering the fine practice of covering the altar only for the eucharistic rite. This provides another ritual gesture for the preparation of the altar, and it allows the communal table to be present in all its strength. Other experiments are ongoing as we strive to find the right covers for our specific tables. Seasonal colors and natural fabrics other than linen can dress the table well, but we are ill-served by polyester.

Several years before Vatican II, the Roman rite dropped the requirement of a frontal or antependium. As altars became free-standing, it became all the more obvious that mandates for decorating only the front should be discontinued. Now *Environment and Art in Catholic Worship* (95) appropriately calls for festive coverings to avoid covering just the facade and to respect the integrity of the furniture. With the expansion of possibilities for altar cloths and their ability to express the given seasons, we are rightly less inclined to use extra hangings (sometimes called paraments) for festivals.

Another current fashion is trite — having the altar cloth or extra hangings match the season's chasuble, stole, ambo cover, lectionary cover, wall hangings and even book ribbons. When matching becomes so relentlessly pervasive, the priest often appears to be a piece of furniture, or the entire environment resembles a jigsaw puzzle or diorama. Each item in the eucharistic assembly place should be chosen with an eye for its compatibility with the space and with other objects — but each also should have its own vitality and form.

CORPORALS

Altar cloths are closely linked to the piece of linen termed the corporal. Related to the Latin term for "body," the corporal always has been an additional altar cloth spread under the eucharistic vessels. Over the centuries, it has shrunk in size and taken on its own identity, although in a few groups, the Carthusians,

After it is washed, anointed with chrism and incensed, the altar is robed in fine linen on its dedication day.
Photo: Regina Kuehn

for example, it continues to resemble an altar cloth. In most churches the corporal came to be considered as different from altar cloths — different in that it was square and small, spread out just before the eucharistic act and folded in on itself just after the action, thereby gathering any eucharistic particles. In its late medieval form, it was carried to and from the altar in a fabric-covered case or envelope called a "burse."

The size for today's corporals should relate to their ritual use and the dimensions of the local altar. Some parishes do not supplement their regular altar cover at all. The *General Instruction of the Roman Missal* continues to indicate that a corporal is spread out as part of the preparation of the altar, as a second altar cover to rest under the eucharistic vessels. Thus the corporal will be measured in feet or yards, not in inches. It will be rolled or folded as befits the size of the altar and the number of eucharistic vessels. The creases once mandated for corporals are no longer required. They related to such now-abrogated rites as resting the host on the corporal and placing the paten under the side of the corporal. The Tridentine understanding of the corporal's purpose was the containment of eucharistic crumbs. Now the corporal also protects the more permanent cover from stains. No burse is mentioned in any of the ritual books; larger corporals usually would not fit in them. Furthermore, corporals should be seen as altar covers, not as private accessories of the chalice.

OTHER COVERS

The credence table, the table holding the bread and wine before the procession of the gifts, and various other occasional tables might benefit from cloth covers. In each case, the need for a cover is to be based on the table's design and placement. If the table is simple, strong and well-designed, it is better left uncovered.

We might also consider the revival of the old custom of covering images and crosses during Lent. Just as we wait in Lent for the water and the light of the Paschal triduum, so too we await the cross. This is why it has long been traditional during Lent either to veil the cross or to store it out of sight. In ancient times the cross, gilded and bejeweled as a sign of victory, would be veiled during penitential seasons. In medieval times, the entire sanctuary was hidden behind the "lenten veil" or "rood screen." We treat music in similar fashion. We give up the Alleluia during Lent only to sing it with great gusto at Easter. In like manner, the veiling of the cross permits us to restore it joyfully at the Triduum. The often-ignored rubric (printed in the sacramentary after the Mass texts for the Saturday of the Fourth Week of Lent) reminds us of these veils.

Local decisions should be made about the best ways to express austerity. The images can be removed or covered, and the processional cross (or other sanctuary cross) can be veiled from the start of Lent or only for the final, more intense, passion-oriented weeks of the season. If any of these veils have been passed on from earlier generations, they are probably violet. New ones may be made of other colors. (*Editor's note: The Bishops' Committee on the Liturgy has recently ruled that the practice of veiling images requires the approval of the national episcopal conference and notes that no such approval has been given.*)

LINENS FOR USE WITH THE CHALICE

The purificator functions as a liturgical napkin. It is used to wipe the lip of the chalice after each communicant partakes of the wine; it is used again for drying wine vessels after they have been cleansed. The expansion of eucharistic cup-sharing has necessitated an increase in purificators. Before the current age of reform, the general practice was for a priest to keep his purificator for several Masses, even for the whole week. Now they are more clearly seen as textiles at the service of the whole community, one purificator per cup per Mass, to be laundered and pressed after each use. Sacristans should make sure that extra purifications are on hand at Easter and Christmas.

Like the other cloths described in this chapter, purificators should be made of white linen. The absorbent qualities of linen (always unstarched) are particularly important for this textile. Perhaps some types of cotton will be durable and absorbent, but probably no synthetic fabric will perform very well as a purificator. Its traditional size is still fitting, as is the old way of folding it — twice on itself, giving triple thickness for enhanced absorbency. If colors other than white are selected, they should not distract communicants. The purpose of the purificator is not the implanting of a whole new symbol but rather the unobtrusive and effective service of the cup of salvation.

Because pall means cover, the word might appear often in the sacristy, denoting the casket pall, the altar cloth that is a pall, any other covering over the ambo or other furniture during Lent or at other times, and a cover for the chalice. The chalice pall is completely optional, but is was formerly seen at every Mass — a stiff square of linen protecting the contents of the chalice from dust and insects. When such a covering is needed today, a purificator or corporal might be placed on the cup. This would actually reflect ancient usage, when part of the top altar cloth was folded up over the cup for such protection.

In the years after Trent, this pall actually came to play a different role. The chalice and paten were prepared before Mass in a fascinating construct: empty chalice, purificator straddling its top and falling to either side, small paten resting over this, and then pall over the paten. Over all this went the chalice veil, followed by the burse containing the corporal. To hold this all together, the pall needed to be more than just a bug-deterring cover for the cup. It became quite thick and starched, or a piece of cardboard was added into a linen pocket to provide a firm base and shape to veil and burse. Now that this whole construct is not only unnecessary but also disadvantageous, the pall need not be a stiff. Older ones still can be used for the few times that bugs might be present, but the ones with excessive ornamentation, especially with fringes of lace, should be retired.

When Catholics looked at the post-Tridentine assemblage of chalice, paten and varied cloths, they mostly saw the chalice veil forming a sort of three-dimensional trapezoid. In some catechetical traditions of a generation or more ago, we were taught that if you came into Mass after the priest took the chalice veil off, then you had come too late to have that Mass "count." Now that we have laid aside such minimalistic attitudes about liturgical participation, and now that we know that the vessels should be seen for what they are, many of us are surprised to hear that chalice veils are still described in the current liturgical books. They are seldom seen in many areas, but here's how the documents say they should be used:

- The chalice, resting before Mass on the credence table, not the altar, is covered with a veil. It can always be white, although it could, according to tradition, be the color of the day (see *General Instruction of the Roman Missal*, 80c). Only at the preparation of the altar is the chalice brought to the altar and filled.

- After communion, the vessels can be purified at the altar or at the credence table. Especially if there are several vessels to be purified after communion (and this is most frequently the case on Sundays in parishes), they can be left "properly covered and on a corporal" either at the altar or (far better) at the credence table. They would then be purified after the assembly has dispersed (see *General Instruction of the Roman Missal*, 120, 138).

The proper cover might be the purificators opened out and spread over the vessels; otherwise, a cloth veil that is large enough to cover all the vessels could be used. If the latter option if followed, this would almost certainly be a larger cover than a chalice veil remaining from a past era. The scale would be more like the humeral veil, although the materials and lining of those stretches of fabric would probably make them too heavy for this function. A larger corporal, perhaps the one taken from the altar, would be more fitting.

TOWELS

Most liturgical towels of earlier years were of fine linen. They were both properly absorbent and unobtrusive. Only those marred by lace or busy embroidery are unfitting candidates for continued use. New towels can be made either of linen or of the other materials now acceptable for liturgical textiles. As with the purificator, however, we should pay close attention to the absorbency of any material we select. Also, there should be some system to keep purificators separate from any similarly sized towels as they are laundered and are put back into their drawers. We need to have at least the following towels at hand:

- towels of a large size for each of the persons involved in the washing of the feet on Holy Thursday. If towels from rectories or other homes are used, they should be plain and of a subdued color so as not to distract anyone from the ongoing rite.

- towels for washing of the hands at Mass (at the preparation rite or after communion). White is traditional; other colors used should be plain and unobtrusive. The vessels and towels should presume the washing of hands, not fingertips.

- towels for drying neophytes: babies, children and adults. Obviously the number will vary from year to year, and the size will be determined by the method of baptism. As adults step from an immersion font, they are best enshrouded in a huge towel.

- a liturgical apron ("gremial") is used by a bishop or his delegate at certain rites to protect vestments from drops of chrism. When called for in the rites, this large linen square or rectangle with strings is supplied by the bishop's office. If not, a large amice can be used.

BANNER BASICS

Judy Kensel Dioszegi

Banners announce a celebration. Through the centuries, pennants, banners and flags have acted as heralds, bearing colors and coats-of-arms and telling the stories of those who create, carry, hang or wave them. Banners can evoke joy, enthusiasm and anticipation, or they can invite silence, meditation and contemplation. They challenge our imaginations and inspire feeling. What better way to set the mood for liturgy? Banners, mobiles and hangings can invite the assembly into its liturgy with form and color.

PRINCIPLES

A prerequisite to designing banners is reading *Environment and Art in Catholic Worship* (EACW), which encourages us in our quest for beauty. "Quality" and "appropriateness" are two of the most important words EACW uses to describe what artists must constantly strive for in their work. "Quality is perceived only by contemplation, by standing back from things and really trying to see them. . . . Contemplation sees the handstamp of the artist, the honesty and care that went into the object's making, the pleasing form and color and texture" (EACW, 20–21). A work of art like a banner is appropriate if it is capable of bearing the weight of mystery and awe evoked by the holy and also serving — not interrupting — the ritual.

SOME DIRECTIVES

That is the aesthetic. Let's state some simple directives. Banners help create a hospitable atmosphere that encourages the assembly to participate and celebrate. Be dedicated to hospitality.

Judy Kensel Dioszegi's nylon mobile for Ordinary Time hangs over the assembly's place at St. Francis de Sales Church, Lake Zurich, Illinois. Note the processional banners in their stands behind the altar.

Photo: Judy Kensel Dioszegi

Know the place for which you are designing the banner. Which areas need attention? Plan color and texture for the whole place, not just the sanctuary. (The experience of hospitality begins in the parking lot. Banners in the parking lot? Why not?)

Simple curved forms thoughtfully designed, or geometric patterns used in moderation, and well-chosen colors interacting with one another are all that are needed to make a successful banner. Remember, the banner's purpose is to contribute to a hospitable environment for liturgy, not to send a bold and blatant message. Let color, form and texture do the talking.

Choose high-quality fabrics. "High quality" doesn't necessarily mean "most expensive." Linens and linen blends work well, as do velvets, corduroys, some cottons and cotton blends. Experiment with putting different kinds of fabric together. Various textures can enhance and complement each other. A few years ago I completed a tapestry triptych measuring eight feet by eight feet, done entirely of heavy woven silks: three distinctly different striated and striped ones, variations on two of these, and a sixth kind of silk with a geometric pattern as background. Integrating them was definitely a challenge, but it worked well.

Don't be afraid to experiment. Make a color scale drawing of the banner using paper and colored markers or pencils, and work with it in the place where the final product will hang. Take time to lay out pattern pieces and change them as you work.

Appliqué—attaching smaller fabric pieces to a larger background—is the most common technique in making banners. Printing a one-of-a-kind banner is usually cost prohibitive. Embroidery is possible for details but probably wouldn't show too well from a distance. With some fabrics—nylon, for example—the background can be cut away and the pieces of the design sewn in, giving the banner a translucent quality—like stained glass—that is quite lovely.

SUSPENDED BANNERS

When making a banner that will be hung from the ceiling or on a wall, pay attention to scale. Make sure that, when suspended,

For the blessed sacrament chapel in the Shrine of Our Lady of the Snows, Belleville, Illinois, Judy Dioszegi created this raw silk triptych. It evokes the northern lights associated with the miracles of Our Lady of the Snows. It also recalls the stained-glass window in the wall behind the altar in the church, linking the reservation with the celebration of the eucharist.

Photo: Judy Kensel Dioszegi

During Ordinary Time at St. Francis de Sales Church, these banners in the narthex give a hint of the mobile hanging in the main body of the church (see page 69).

Photo: Judy Kensel Dioszegi

the banner doesn't create a visual barrier. Also, notice how lighting affects it. Do you want light to shine through the banner? If so, use sheer fabrics — chiffon, curtain scrim or nylon. If the banner needs to be made taut, insert a wooden dowel or a length of lightweight aluminum rod into a pocket. Consider, though, the lovely possibilities of subtle movement when suspended banners hang freely.

PROCESSIONAL BANNERS

Banners designed to be carried in procession need to be light enough to be carried. Use polyvinyl chloride (PVC) pipes in the top and bottom hems, and lightweight wooden poles. When choosing fabric, pay attention to how it will move when carried. Is it attractive on both sides? (Both sides will be visible.) Consider attaching bells to the banner. Carefully plan where the banners will be placed when not being carried in procession. If they are to be placed in view, make sure that they stand straight.

OUTDOOR BANNERS

Permanent outdoor banners require special consideration and construction. Seasonal or special occasion banners to be hung or carried outdoors are relatively simple to make. Follow the tips above. Quick-drying, brightly colored nylon works well. Check

for colorfastness. Banners that hang against exterior walls may bleed and discolor wood or brick when drenched. Pay careful attention to scale. Look at light posts, arches, doorways, fence posts and maybe even tree branches for possible locations.

A CHALLENGE

In *Parish Path through Lent and Eastertime* (Chicago: Liturgy Training Publications, 1985), John Buscemi challenges artists "to help create an environment in which people are nurtured. The people of God are fed by the visual arts. . . . Through the arts, the members of the assembly can experience the place in which they gather as one which reveres creation, helps share burdens through signs of welcome, and, finally, calls the assembly to praise God with thanksgiving." So as artists, we are challenged to offer our own unique creations. Let us craft carefully and to the best of our abilities. Let us always work from out of prayer, because that is how talent comes to us — and through us to our assemblies.

— ◎ ◎ ◎ —

*Figure 1. The All Saints banner by Norman Laliberté is composed
of smaller individual panels, each depicting a saint.*
Photo: Mark Scott

Figure 2. Notice the draping effect of the fabric and the limited palette of colors that Laliberté used here.
Photo: Mike Scott

◆— ◎ ◎ ◎ —◆

Figure 3. The pregnant Virgin, shown in silhouette, looks dated today but was quite provocative when it was created in the early 1960s.
Photo: Mark Scott

Figure 4. Laliberté's depiction of the crucifixion is folk-like in design. Like many children's drawings, the simplicity cuts through sentimentality to the heart of the mystery.
Photo: Mark Scott.

‣— ◎ ◎ ◎ —‣

A mat woven of vegetable fibers looks as rich as a carpet but is not damaged by water splashed from this font. Church at Burnham Norton, Norfolk, England. Photo: Regina Kuehn

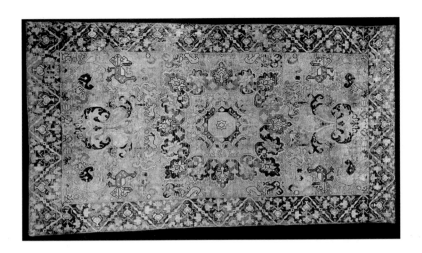

PRAYER CARPETS

David Philippart

In the church's house, textiles are used primarily to clothe people and the altar. Yet they adorn the building too, not only overhead but also underfoot. Some Native Americans had special animal skins on which they prayed. Muslims have a long tradition of using prayer carpets. And medieval Christians in the colder climates of northern Europe began dressing the floors of cold stone churches with vegetable fiber mats as well as fabric rugs. Instead of monotonous, wall-to-wall carpeting, a well-chosen, strategically placed carpet can add color and texture to the room as it honors the altar or defines a place for devotion in a shrine.

LEARNING FROM LALIBERTÉ

Mark Scott

An artist who contributed greatly to the renaissance of the banner is Norman Laliberté. He received his master of science degree from the Illinois Institute of Technology and has taught at St. Mary's College in Notre Dame, Indiana, and at the Rhode Island School of Design. Laliberté received a great deal of notoriety when he was commissioned to do a set of 88 banners for the Vatican Pavilion at the 1964 World's Fair in New York. (Those banners eventually made their way to Rockefeller Chapel at the University of Chicago, where they are displayed occasionally.) Other commissions soon followed: in Chicago, for Northwestern University Hospital and the Civic Opera House, and for corporations and private individuals around the country.

Laliberté's work has a sophisticated playfulness, and his images sometimes border on the exotic. He uses a wide range of textiles and fabrics, and patterns and solids, to give his banners a layered richness and depth. He allows the material to be itself, permitting it to wrinkle and drape, giving the surface of the banner a liveliness that cannot be mistaken for any medium other than cloth. He respects the intrinsic nature of his medium, working honestly with it to create something new.

The four examples pictured on pages 73 – 75 are from the set of banners commissioned for the Vatican Pavilion. Figures 1 and 2 show the explosion of color that sometimes characterizes his work. The banners are constructed from many individually designed squares — in figure 1, the faces of the saints, and in figure 2, various symbols. Both designs have a quilt-like feel to them. The banner for All Saints (figure 1) has a wide range of color; the banner in figure 2 has a limited palette. In both cases, though, the folds and draping of the fabric add a liveliness to the design that gives the work a richness and weight.

Both of these banners capitalize on an idea that easily could be adapted by a group of people — such as a religion class, for instance — wishing to make a banner. Each member would be responsible for a small section, and then the sections would be assembled to create the final work. Different styles would complement each other. Harmony could be achieved by the careful arrangement of the pieces by someone with some design competency. Weakly designed sections would be bolstered by the more prominent placement of the stronger ones.

Figures 3 and 4 show Laliberté's use of representational images. Figure 3 depicts that fantastic Advent oxymoron — the pregnant virgin. Here, Mary is silhouetted, showing her physical condition, which becomes a symbol for the expectancy and anticipation of Advent. Laliberté takes the anticipation of that great cosmic event, the Incarnation, and presents it in very human terms, the impending birth of a child. He takes an abstract concept and through representation allows us to relate to it on a level at which most of us have had some experience. (While the figure of Mary, with her ponytail and high-heeled shoes, may look dated to us, and the notion of depicting her as pregnant strikes us today as nothing new, imagine the impact that the image must have had in 1964!)

The banner of the crucifixion (figure 4) is almost folklike or primitive in its design. The theology of the death of Christ is presented in the strong, simple image of blood flowing into the cups held high by believers. Like many children's drawings, the stark simplicity cuts through any sentimentality to the heart of the matter and to the core of the mystery.

Laliberté's works teach us that banner-making can indeed be a noble craft and that good banners are appropriate for use in liturgical worship. No longer do we need to settle for quickly fabricated cloth signs. Following his example, contemporary textile artists can create for our time within a timeless medium, a medium of richness and depth, color and texture that evokes the numinous.

WORKING WITH A WEAVER

Lynn Lautz

How does a parish work with a designer/weaver to procure vestments, paraments or hangings? Speaking as a liturgical fiber artist (yarn and fabric being my mediums), I would describe the process as one of great sharing between the community and the artist.

The work I create is done on commission. This means that the design (developed between the community and myself), the technique, the materials to be used, the cost and the completion date are agreed upon before I purchase any materials for a project. Most of my work is hand-woven, though I also have done a number of appliqué and quilted processional banners and hangings. What follows is based on my experience. It is an artist's viewpoint of the nature of this work and of the church-artist relationship.

WHAT DOES A FIBER ARTIST CREATE?

Any item of cloth (however made) that is used in the worship space can be viewed as fiber work for the liturgy. This includes vestments (items worn by people), paraments (items used in conjunction with the furniture of the space), hangings (permanent, seasonal or for special events) and processional banners. Permanent pieces are those pieces normally present in the space; seasonal pieces may be used over many years but are present only during those feasts or seasons for which they were designed; works designed for special events are temporary, usually used just once or perhaps just for rare occasions.

WHY WORK WITH A FIBER ARTIST?

The pieces created by an artist are unique, one-of-a-kind items. In an age when so many things are mass produced, to seek and purchase an artist's work says something about caring and involvement. By commissioning work, a community is able to obtain a product designed and created especially for its own particular setting. This is very different from shopping in a store or catalog or even purchasing a piece from an exhibit. The commissioning process begins with needs, ideas and imagination, all shared and understood together. The process between client and artist then relies on good communication and mutual trust.

FINDING A WEAVER

Most of my clients come by referral. Often someone has seen my work in a church, religious center or school and locates me through these contacts. Sometimes I am recommended by an architect or liturgical consultant and occasionally by a news article. Any parish considering commissioning an artist's work, then, should alert committee members and perhaps others to keep their eyes open, to ask questions and to visit other communities known to have sought out artists in the past. Other sources for locating artists include registries, galleries (people in galleries may be the ones to tell you about registries of artists), local guilds, various supply stores that deal in the raw materials for artists and craftspeople, and craft organizations. Periodicals aimed at artists may be of great assistance. Clients for art in any medium need to know these sources and others in the local and regional area.

Working with an artist before and through a commission requires far more involvement and time than does purchasing an existing piece of art. Finding possible artists and making a selection is itself a time-consuming process, but this involvement invariably adds another level of meaning to the project.

PROJECT DURATION

In my experience, the nature of the work determines the project's duration. Large tapestries or a full set of vestments or paraments often take a year form the time of first contact to the actual completion of the project. I design all of my own work and use no more than two other artisans to help produce it. Larger studios may assign more people to a project, but the quantity of work done by these studios may offset any significant time savings. In general, project time will vary among artists and should be something that all agree about at the beginning of the process.

COST

Probably the largest variable in artistic work is the renumeration. I use guidelines for estimating based on my own style, location, financial expectations and overhead. For example: A basically plain weave (wool, rayon and/or linen) project might be around $35 per square foot, but if silk is used or if hand dyeing of the yarns is necessary, then $45 is a better figure; tapestry work is more likely to be $60-$70 per square foot; stoles tend to be $100 or more each, but if woven in double cloth (which can allow for some design interplay), $200 each is more likely. These costs include the work being interlined and lined, ready to hang and use when the client receives it. Again, these are my own guidelines and should not be applied to other artists' work. What matters is that cost be discussed very early.

The installation of hangings may also affect the total cost, especially for high or otherwise difficult locations. Some artists want a role in the installation, as this can be vital to the success of the work. If so, this needs to become a part of the contract and should be so stated in the agreement. Large pieces or difficult locations may require paid installers or special equipment.

Other possible costs might come in having the artist present for the dedication, in the preparation of information about the work commissioned and in storage and transportation. Materials, time and travel expenses over and above the cost of actually producing the commissioned piece may well be warranted.

How does a community pay for art? Memorials are a common means of funding, or at least of starting a fund. Other contributions will come from those committed to the notion that the church needs art and artists. Sometimes (but not often enough) art is included in the budget of a new building or a renovation. Rarely (what a revolution it would be to see change here), art is written into the yearly budget of a parish; the budgeted amount may need to be enhanced by memorials and donations, but the basic parish commitment is there. One important factor is this: Generally, people like to know what they are giving for, so a demonstrated need coupled with a good design can go a long way toward securing the needed funds.

THE COMMISSIONING PROCESS

First there is an initial contact — usually a call or letter expressing interest in my work. For new clients, I propose a meeting between myself and the committee or persons responsible for the projects. At this meeting the potential client can view slides and samples of my past work, discuss the commissioning process and explore the artistic ideas to be developed. The meeting is best held at the project's site so that we can see and talk about the environment. For fiber art, it is important at this point to see what yarn colors and various fabrics look like in the actual location. Lighting, both natural and electric, greatly affects the color. I photograph the space and make notes on the colors of wood, carpet, art glass and any other permanent architectural features. Finally, we decide who the contact person should be, the one individual who is to act as liaison between the artist and the parish's committee. It is most important from both sides that both communication and accountability be resolved.

This part of the process is somewhat different when the community uses an art consultant instead of or in addition to the parish committee. This initial meeting with the artist may then be with the consultant alone.

Following the initial meeting, I develop a color drawing of my proposal. Again, it is best when the proposal can be viewed and discussed at the project's location. Other design-related information that must be dealt with includes materials, costs and time required for completion. When the design is approved, an agreement can be written. I send this agreement along with yarn samples to the contact person. When I receive back a signed agreement and a one-third down payment, the yarns are ordered and work begins.

Throughout the project, the parish committee needs to attend to communication within the community itself. The church bulletin or newsletter may carry items about the project and its progress. Members of the parish like being kept informed, and their anticipation will increase the excitement and appreciation of the art at the final installation.

COMPLETING THE WORK

I use color, lines, shape and textures in my work (not words) to invite participation. I want viewers to be drawn in and to interpret what they see. I start with ideas and create a design imbued with certain meanings, but it is amazing to hear the depth, breadth and variety of viewers' understandings. With weaving especially, one sees the overall colors from afar, but as one comes closer, more detail and nuances are seen. It is this kind of involvement which I believe is essential for fiber art in a worship setting. We experience our environment through all our senses: what we see, hear, touch, taste and smell. All shape our perception of an event.

Ideally, cloth in worship defines roles, creates focal points, unites action and environment, and even helps the participants open themselves to greater understanding and involvement. Meaning here is something that grows. It is not fixed by the artist but develops over the years with the community's using, handling and looking and their remembering all the times and deeds in this place, in the presence of this assembly.

CARE OF FIBER ART

Under normal circumstances and climates, permanent hangings and tapestries need to be vacuumed once a year. Some highly textured tapestries may collect dust more quickly and require vacuuming every six months. Vestments and paraments need dry cleaning only when they are soiled; it is a good idea to clean the entire set at the same time. Be aware that fading and accelerated deterioration can result from prolonged exposure to sunlight for some types of fiber pieces.

Storing fiber art in plastic is not recommended. Natural fibers attract moisture; when the plastic traps this moisture, mildew is possible. Folding fabric on the same creases every time can cause needless wear. The best way to store large fabric pieces is to roll them. Cardboard tubes covered with muslin make good rolling forms; clean sheets provide fine final coverings. Another way to store larger pieces involves hanging the muslin-covered tubes with ropes from the ceiling, then draping the hangings from them and covering the hangings with a clean sheet.

LONGEVITY

Some tapestries are hundreds of years old. With ordinary use, hand-woven work can be expected to last several decades. Check on the items now used to discover when they were purchased and how they are to be cleaned. Maintain ongoing records of such matters as use, care, storage and location.

THE TEXTILES OF NANCY CHINN

THE ARTIST'S STATEMENT

I am a painter and textile artist by training and by nature. About sixteen years ago, I was transfixed by the contributions of non-Christian visual artists to their respective faith communities. In contrast, I found within my own Christian tradition that the contemporary contribution of visual artists was almost non-existent, decorative at best, relying on sentimentality, familiarity, romanticism and narrative content to carry the work. This was not enough for me. I had a vision of creating art within community, with the members' participation in design, execution and installation.

Ephemeral materials and methods proclaim the presence of God in a particular moment for a particular community. I see my work like that of the choir, the readers, the presider: bound in a temporal format. I weave together liturgy as my warp and

Above: Nancy Chinn's <u>Tree of Life</u> is a series of hand-cut, paper-lace hangings. Each piece is 9'x36'. The ensemble hung in 1991 over the font at Grace Cathedral (Episcopal), San Francisco.
Photo: Nancy Chinn

art as my weft. I push the materials until the art has power beyond what its individual elements can do alone.

This style of making art requires close coordination with those in the community responsible for leading worship. A work of art has sensate potential as well as theological and ethical components. I find that the questions that I raise in seeking that component are what is needed to move a work from a vague abstraction toward an increased clarity in understanding our lives as a community and as individuals. Art comes from the nonrational part of our spirits, not the cognitive functions. It is important when planning a work of art for the place of worship, and when preparing the rites and music of worship as well, to take time to brood, to allow things to gestate.

Tongues of Fire, Mighty Wind
is created from 50 pieces
of painted nylon net, each 18
inches wide but varying in
length from 20 feet to 120
feet. The painting process
involved dipping the net in a
mixture of acrylic pigment,
medium and water. The
pieces were then laid out to
dry. The work is illuminated
by existing light fixtures.

Photo: Nancy Chinn

The 50 pieces of <u>Tongues of Fire, Mighty Wind</u> were first hung improvisationally by three people on the catwalks 92 feet above the floor. The artist directed from below, and three more people assisted from the floor in tying the pieces. There are two anchor points. The overall dimensions are approximately 200' x 50'.

Photo: Nancy Chinn

THE TEXTILES OF CATHERINE KAPIKIAN

THE ARTIST'S STATEMENT

My work is site specific. It is empowered by community and created on behalf of community. Visual theological proclamation must be accompanied by education. This process is a collaborative responsibility shared by the artist, the parish's or institution's committee and the pastoral staff. Such a process helps a community to comprehend better the space itself, the nonverbal vocabulary of the visual and the wisdom of sponsoring and contemplating images that communicate evocatively and with nuance rather than heavy-handedly illustrating or merely decorating. The process of comprehending a work of art, like the process of creating the work itself, is a time of joy.

To that end, what follows are some notes toward comprehending specific works that I have done.

89

These Pentecost banners are one of six sets of seasonal hangings designed by Catherine Kapikian and fabricated by members of Immaculate Conception Church, Towson, Maryland, in 1984. The dimensions of each banner are 7' x 3'. "The banners," the artist explains, "function like a visual trumpet blast."

Photo: Catherine Kapikian

Revelation 22:1 — 21 is a
wood and fiber installation
created by Catherine
Kapikian in 1991 for the hall
in Falls Church Presbyterian
Church in Falls Church,
Virginia. (Above, complete
installation; left, a detail.)
It replaces the curtain on the
hall stage. Each of the
four units has two hinged
parts, and the units can
be used independently around
the room to create spaces
for small groups.

The river of life flows from
the Lamb of God on the
throne in the new Jerusalem.
Evil — the red monster — is
turned upside down and nips
at the angels.

Photos: Catherine Kapikian

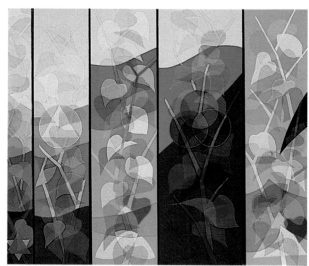

Catherine Kapikian designed these panels to complete a wood reredos (37' x7') in Prince of Peace Lutheran Church, Alexandria, Virginia. Above are the Advent panels, evoking the inbreaking of the reign of God. At right are the panels for the time after Pentecost ("Ordinary Time" for Roman Catholics). The unifying device in all the sets of these panels — these are the only two sets completed to date — is the imagery of flowing water. The panels are wool appliqué.

Photos: Catherine Kapikian

HANGING BANNERS AND MOBILES
A MATTER OF BALANCE

John Dioszegi

Over the years I have seen some truly lovely banners—hung by twine tied haphazardly to a broom handle sticking out much more than was necessary from the top pocket. Hanging a banner is a very small part of the job. However, if as much love and care as was devoted to making the banner is not devoted to hanging it, its beauty is diminished. Because my wife is a fabric artist, we have had the opportunity to create many banners and mobiles for religious and commercial applications. This chapter is a review of our experience with hanging banners and with making armatures for mobiles.

A general rule to bear in mind when making the hanger for a banner: If the top rod is to be flush with the width of the textile, *make sure that it is flush with the edge*. If it sticks out ⅛- or ¼-inch, it can be distracting. In some cases, it may be desirable to have the top rod extend beyond the edge. But then finish it tastefully, perhaps with finials or the like.

DOWELS

When wooden dowels are used to hang banners, ¾-inch is the minimum diameter to use. Even under the load of a light banner, dowels of smaller diameters will bend, causing the banner to hang unevenly. If a simple, plain end cut is desired, sand the cut smooth. Finish the dowel with paint, stain, varnish or a clear coating as desired.

There are various ways of using different types of hardware to suspend banners using wooden dowels. Figure 1 shows the

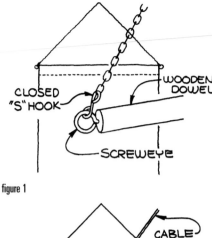

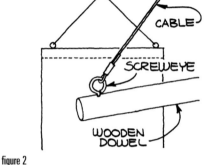

figure 1

figure 2

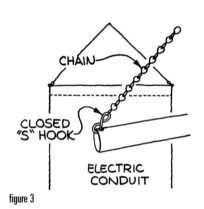

figure 3

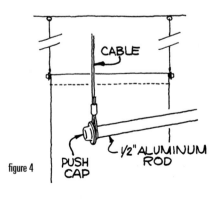

figure 4

use of a screweye at the end of the dowel. The advantage here is that the hardware does not pierce the fabric. Figure 2 shows the placement of the screweye on top of the dowel. While this necessitates piercing the fabric, such an arrangement, when hung overhead, leaves the screweye barely visible, if at all.

An S-hook, closed with a pair of pliers after inserted in place, and lightweight chain can be added to the screweye (figure 1). Or cable can be looped through the screweye and fastened with a swedge (figure 2). For a discussion of what kind of cable to use, see the section in this chapter on mobiles.

ELECTRIC CONDUIT OR ALUMINUM ROD

If using electrical conduit with S-hooks and chain (figure 3), be sure the end cuts are square. Often when cutting metal conduit and drilling holes in it for hooks, a very sharp burr or edge results, capable of cutting hands or fabric. Always file the ends square and smooth, and remove any burrs. We have found ½-inch aluminum rod (not tubing) to be light, strong and adaptable to our needs. The ends can be finished with chrome-plated push caps. The push caps create a barrier to help center the fabric on the rod, and they hold the looped cable ends used as hangers (figure 4). Instead of using looped cable, it is possible to drill through the rod and fasten the cable using a swedge or stop (figure 5).

SINGLE-POINT SUSPENSION

When suspending a dowel or rod from a single point, locate and drill

94

the exact balance point so that the banner hangs perfectly. That point may not be in the exact center of the dowel because some banner designs have much more material sewn on one side than on the other. Nothing is more distracting to some people than a slightly crooked picture or a slightly out-of-kilter banner.

Drilling through the rod and running cable through it ensures that the top hem will not bunch up over a loop of cable or chain. Fasten the cable with a swedge or stop underneath the rod. Slitting the back of the pocket will make assembly easier (figure 6).

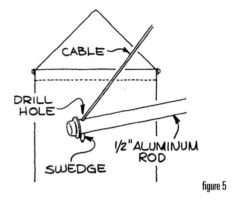

figure 5

BOTTOM HEM SUPPORT

Some banners are designed to have a soft, loose, free-form bottom edge. Others may look better with a sharp, straight, tailored appearance. Such banners need a stiffener in a bottom hem. Use a piece of ½-inch aluminum rod. It is small enough in diameter so as not to be noticeable and will not warp as wooden dowels of the same size are prone to do.

MOBILES

A mobile is a free-moving, three-dimensional piece of art suspended in space. It is composed of a group of balanced, interconnected arms with objects suspended from those arms. The suspended objects are the main focus. The armature exists to present them.

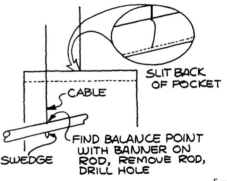

figure 6

The action of mobiles has always fascinated me. One element moves, and the entire structure reacts. One action of one part affects the entire mechanism. At a deep, spiritual level the movement of a mobile says a great deal about life and living. If one sits and contemplates a mobile, unusual things often happen within one's consciousness. A mobile's gentle motion almost compels one to watch it. Yet that very compulsion often frees the mind to be more receptive to inspiration, either from the ambo or beyond. It is altogether fitting and proper for a mobile to be hung in church.

The many-armed apparatus that holds Judy Dioszegi's mobile in the Britannica Center in Chicago is a study in balance.

Photo: Judy Kensel Dioszegi

ARMATURE

There are two things of equal importance to consider when making armature. First is its appearance, the aesthetics of its construction. Second is its structural integrity — is it strong enough to hold up the objects it is designed for? Also, it should be assumed that banners, regardless of how and where they are hung, will be changed periodically to reflect the colors of the natural and/or liturgical seasons. Therefore, it is advisable to install a winch and pulley system in order to be able to raise and lower the mobile. Installation is often an expensive procedure employing a scaffold or a high lift to gain access to the ceiling locations of the pulleys. But it saves work when it's time to change the banners. For the initial want of a few dollars, it makes no sense to have to replace an inexpensive pulley that fails. Buy only high-quality materials for all parts of the mechanism. It's most cost-effective.

CABLE

Local governments often have specific regulations about things hanging over people's heads in public places. In Chicago, for example, a safety factor of at least 5 is required of all elements of anything suspended over the heads of people. If a mobile weighs 60 pounds — fabric, armature and hardware — the cable, pulleys and anchorage must be able to support 5 times 60, or 300 pounds. In our installations, the safety factor for the lifting mechanism is often well over a factor of 50. Since the armatures I make are wood or aluminum and therefore reasonably light for their size, a very small cable *could* be used and still meet the safety factor of 5. But smaller diameter cables can easily kink or jump out of the pulley or groove. I therefore often use much heavier cable.

Regardless of the weight of the mobile, the *minimum* size cable I use is 7 x 7 x 3/32-inch galvanized steel aircraft cable with a breaking strength of 920 pounds. The cable I use is also vinyl-coated to help prevent kinking. If a mobile weighed only 30 pounds, I still would use this kind of cable even though a 1/32-inch cable would meet safety factor specifications. When fabricating cable to hardware, always use the appropriate size cables, swedges and a swedging tool to make the attachment. This means that the hem or pocket must be large enough to accommodate it (figure 7). And swedges should only be used on bare cable; remove the vinyl coating on the section of cable being swedged.

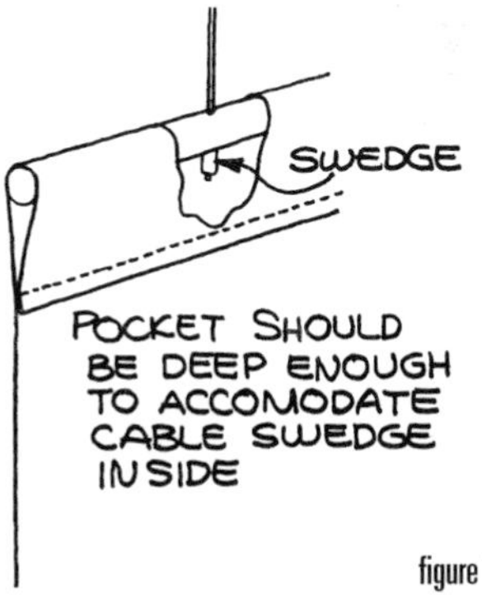

SWIVEL JOINTS

The installation of a mobile without a swivel joint between the cable and an individual arm is dangerous. The winding and unwinding of the cable, caused by the revolutions of the mobile, weakens the cable and could possibly break it. Mobiles by definition involve free movement. Therefore, a ball bearing swivel joint, with a safety factor of at least 5, should be installed between cable and individual arm. I have used 500-pound test ball bearing fishing swivels for light-weight installations (30 pounds or less). Though the manufacturer has issued a disclaimer freeing it from responsibility in the case of injury or damage due to the failure of its swivel when used in a mobile, the 500-pound fishing swivels have proven more than suitable for under 30 pounds of mobile. For installations over 30 pounds, I use an industrial, angular contact ball bearing swivel with a working load of 900 pounds. It is expensive but should be used for safety.

SWEDGE

POCKET SHOULD BE DEEP ENOUGH TO ACCOMODATE CABLE SWEDGE INSIDE

figure 7

Viewed from the floor, the armature is an integral part of the design of the mobile. Here, form follows function, but function includes not only holding up the mobile but being beautiful and integral, too.

Photo: Judy Kensel Dioszegi

THE ARMS

Though the arms of a mobile may be made from many materials (wood, fiberglass, plastic or metal), I have always used top-grade white pine or aluminum. Pine is light, strong and workable. I take the time to choose only pine with a tight, straight grain, as parallel as possible to the edges of the board. I have spent as much as four hours going through the available supply of wood at the lumber yard in order to get the right pieces. Wood with knots should never be used. When the strength of the arms is in doubt, I fabricate them and actually test them by applying a weight 5 times the weight that the particular arm is supposed to support. It is important, if for no other reason than the peace of mind that comes from knowing that the arm is safe. After shaping and testing the arms, I finish the wood in the traditional manner—fine sanding, sealing, sanding again, painting or staining, and a final coat of clear finish over the stain.

FULCRUMS

Balancing the elements of a mobile is relatively simple. If the mobile will only utilize the original set of banners designed for it, fixed fulcrums may be used. However, since most mobiles for church will be designed to use various sets of banners for various seasons, adjustable fulcrums are needed. This is important in order to rebalance the mobile for each set of banners.

The fulcrum may be fabricated a number of ways; it must be strong enough to do its job. For lightweight installations, I use interconnecting eyebolts with stainless steel strapping around the edge of the arm for reinforcement (figure 8). For heavier installations, I have used ¼-inch steel rods, designed and threaded for the particular application. Linked eyebolts will allow interconnected arms only limited movement. For full movement of interconnected arms, a swivel joint is required.

Aesthetically, it is generally desirable to have a space between the banners and the armature. Banners that appear to float free in space are always interesting. To accomplish this effect, suspend each banner from the armature with cable. A 300-pound test, ball-bearing fishing swivel inserted between the cable and the armature allows full, free motion to the suspended banner. Though banners weigh a few pounds at most, the 300-pound swivel is desirable for its durability. I have installed smaller swivels and have had to replace them because they jammed.

BALANCE

Once designed, constructed and safety tested, the unit has to be installed. This means balancing the mobile. The object in

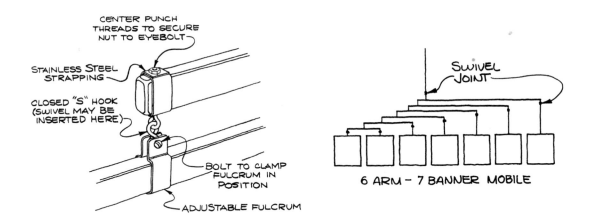

CENTER PUNCH
THREADS TO SECURE
NUT TO EYEBOLT

STAINLESS STEEL
STRAPPING

CLOSED "S" HOOK
(SWIVEL MAY BE
INSERTED HERE)

BOLT TO CLAMP
FULCRUM IN
POSITION

ADJUSTABLE FULCRUM

SWIVEL
JOINT

6 ARM - 7 BANNER MOBILE

balancing is to position the fulcrums so that each arm is itself balanced and parallel to all other arms. With a 12-arm mobile, this might seem complicated. But as with all tasks that seem insurmountable, the trick is to divide the larger task into smaller steps. In balancing any multiple-arm mobile, begin with the bottom arm (figure 9). There is no need to know mathematical formulas or college physics. It is a simple process.

First attach the fulcrum to the arm. Then attach two banners, one at each end. Shift the fulcrum to a position where the arm is balanced in a horizontal position. Once balanced, tighten the fulcrum so that it does not move. The first arm, with its two banners, becomes the load for the second arm. The third banner becomes the second load at the other end of the second arm. Shift the fulcrum until banner three balances the lowest arm with its two banners. Then tighten the second fulcrum. Attach the third fulcrum; adjust it on the third arm so that the fourth banner balances the combined weight of the first and second arms with their banners; then tighten the fulcrum. Continue until all arms are connected and balanced. Then hoist the unit to its position overhead. Only then can you fully appreciate the beauty of your efforts.

CARING FOR THE CHURCH'S VESTURE

Mickey Wright

As vestments, hangings, festal banners, altar cloths and linens, textiles have had an important role in liturgy throughout the history of the church. Since the very nature of liturgical textiles implies *permanence,* we are concerned here with their care. While few parishes today have the vast treasuries of vestments that existed in some medieval churches, the parish treasury of liturgical garments nonetheless must be properly cared for.

CARE OF VESTMENTS

The care of, or to be more specific, the *conservation* and *preservation* of, liturgical garments can be either quite simple or extremely elaborate. Light, dust and stress (or weight) are the three most harmful agents to vestments (or any textile). Older churches usually had (and many still have) specially designed shelving units of wide, shallow drawers that allowed the vestments to be stored flat, thereby reducing any stress caused by hanging the heavily embroidered and jeweled garments. This storage method is the primary reason why many major European and American museums have such spectacular examples of liturgical vestments. Such drawers allowed the garments to be stored not only without stress but also without exposure to light or extreme temperature fluctuations. Without exception, this would still be the storage method of choice.

If one were fortunate enough to be able to construct such a unit (or to have an existing one in place), it would be very simple to protect the garments properly. The vestments should be laid on either sheets of acid-free tissue or unbleached muslin that has been washed to remove any sizing (old bedsheets are fine). Any folds in the garments, as at the shoulders, should be padded with cardboard tubes (preferably acid-free) that have been wrapped in acid-free tissue, or with a cotton batting, such as mattress padding. The garment should then be covered with either acid-free tissue or muslin. If it is necessary to place more than one garment in a drawer, each one should be wrapped separately. If size dictates that the garment must be folded (most sacristy drawers were designed for the old "fiddle-backed" chasubles), the folds must be padded as well.

What if you do not have a wonderful vestment storage unit but have instead that modern innovation, the closet, or even less than that, the "space for hanging" in the sacristy? If vestments must be hung, they can be adequately protected. Throw away the wire coat hangers and invest in the best, sturdiest wooden hangers available. Cover these hangers with cotton batting and then wrap the batting with strips of muslin. This will not only reduce stress at the shoulders but will also help prevent slippage.

While you are throwing away the wire coat hangers, also throw away the plastic bags. Textiles are natural fibers, either plant or animal (polyester does not enter into this discussion — we are not concerned about preserving it!), and must be allowed to breathe. By sealing the garment in plastic, one is virtually smothering it while preventing any moisture from escaping. Ideally, "slipcovers," bags with ample space, sewn from washed, unbleached muslin, could be made for each garment. This prevents dust and light from harming the garment but still allows it to breathe. A simple solution would be muslin yardage, long enough to cover the garment, with a slit at the top for the hanger to protrude. Again, an old bedsheet would work for this. It is important that garments be allowed to "air out" after each wearing and that they not be crowded into the closet. It would be better to have additional rods in the sacristy than to crowd and crease the garments in a small closet.

If possible, keep light away from the vestments. Any light — natural, incandescent or fluorescent — causes fading and fiber breakdown. Drawers protect exceptionally well. The muslin coverings are not total light barriers; they still allow enough light to enter to cause fading and deterioration after a time. If the closet has glass doors (wonderful to see into, but you've covered everything with muslin anyway), cover them with dark cloth or paper. If you have no closet, set up screens and use lower wattage light bulbs in the storage areas to keep the light levels at a minimum.

Folding stoles causes creases. These will, over time, cause the fibers to break down. Roll stoles on acid-free cardboard tubes that have been covered with acid-free tissue, and then wrap them with either tissue or muslin.

It is not difficult to care properly for vestments, and it can be relatively inexpensive. The rewards are many: Costly vestments last for many years, wrinkles and creases disappear, and dry cleaning bills diminish.

CARE OF BANNERS AND HANGINGS

Permanent hangings are those that are constantly on display in the church and have been installed as an integral part of the worship space. In medieval times, that meant large woven tapestries. Churches may have similar tapestries today, but the more common types of church hangings are large fiber/fabric constructions. The conservation/preservation of these large and often elevated works of art can be problematic. Technically, there should be no such thing as a "permanent" hanging. The life of a hanging is drastically shortened when it is displayed for years and when little attention is paid to its care. This often happens. People say, "We have it, we've paid a fortune for it, and we're going to show it forever." Or, "It would take four people and a crane to get it down." How should these large pieces be cared for?

As the first step in lengthening the life of a hanging, turn down the lights! Bright lights, especially strong spotlights, are lethal to fibers of all kinds. They make the fibers brittle and cause the dyes to fade. Textiles in a museum setting are illuminated with between five and seven footcandles of light (a footcandle is the amount of light given off by a standard candle at a distance of one foot.) This sounds like very little light, but it is more than sufficient. The amount of light on your hangings can be measured with a light meter (a light meter can be rented at many photographic equipment stores). If you decide that you must have more light than five to seven footcandles, you can raise the light level with some knowledge of the consequences and use restraint.

Dirt is the other danger to textiles that are hung; dust collects on them constantly. (Think of draperies at spring cleaning time.) The "out-of-sight, out-of-mind" theory often operates very well for hangings that are ten feet or more overhead. They should be taken down at least twice a year, laid flat and carefully vacuumed with the soft brush attachment of a vacuum cleaner. Put a sheet of fiberglass screening (available at hardware stores) over the hanging so as not to disturb the weave or stitching. If the hangings cannot be taken down, get up on a ladder and very carefully vacuum them in place. Unfortunately, the worst types of grime — candle smoke and heating fumes — cannot be vacuumed away and continually build up on the hanging.

Temporary hangings are those hangings that are changed often in the course of a liturgical year — banners, altar frontals, lectern hangings, etc. The most important concern here is not cleaning but storage (how to care properly for those objects not on view). There is only one word for storage: ROLL. Never fold a banner or an altar cloth. The wrinkles from folding will not come out, even with repeated ironings.

The optimum method of storage is to roll the items on acid-free tubes that have been wrapped with acid-free tissue (see sidebar). In the absence of acid-free tubes, use any tube that is several inches longer than the width of the item. Pad the tube (metal or plastic pipe, broom stick, whatever) with cotton batting and roll the textile with the *decorated side OUT*. This is most important for appliquéd works where rolling with the decorated side in will cause distortion, rippling and buckling. Wrap the rolled-up item with muslin and tie it snugly (but not too tightly) with cloth tape or torn strips of muslin. An index card identifying the item can be attached to the tape.

If all this sounds like a lot of trouble to take for old banners and other textiles, consider using this time to do an inventory and to decide that some pieces are expendable. Maybe a rule such as "if we have not used it in five years, we never will" would be helpful. Keep and properly preserve what the parish uses regularly.

When storing the rolled and wrapped banners, lay them horizontally in a single layer to avoid excessive pressure and weight. If space prohibits this kind of storage, stand the rolls on end or stack them, but be particularly careful that there is sufficient ventilation for the rolls to breathe.

WASHABLE TEXTILES

Regularly used and in need of diligent upkeep are altar cloths, corporals, purificators and albs. Traditionally, these items have been made from linen, whose fibers come from the stems of the flax plant and whose use can be dated to 4800 BCE in Egypt. Linen is extremely strong and supple and lends itself to very fine weaves. It has been highly treasured, used and worn by the nobility. Linen thus became the fiber to adorn the sacrificial tables and later the altars of Christians.

Altar cloths today often are still made from linen fiber because of its durability and beauty, although many are now made of cotton or linen/cotton blended with polyester. The problems encountered in cleaning these items are similar to those faced by the host cleaning up after a dinner party: oil and wine stains and candle wax drippings on a prized linen tablecloth. But the stains on church textiles are made more difficult by the factor of time. While the host can take care of spots, stains and drips immediately after the party, the spots, stains and drips in church are rarely attended to on the day they occur. Most sit for a week or more. Obviously, stain removal would be much simpler if linens could be changed and washed on Sunday night or on Monday morning. The longer stains are permitted to set (and this is especially true of stains from red wine, for it acts as a fabric dye on linen fibers), the more difficult they are to remove.

For oil stains (such as chrism) and greasy stains (such as lipstick on purificators), spray the stain with an oil-dissolving prewash spray such as *Shout* or *Spray 'n' Wash*. Then wash in hot water with good-quality laundry detergent (a biodegradable one will do). Altar linens are usually white, and so the hottest water can be used without damage. But make sure you know the cloth is linen or cotton and not a blend with polyester — extremely hot water will damage polyester.

Wine stains, as stated earlier, are easy to remove if treated quickly. Sponging with club soda will usually remove fresh wine stains. White wine applied to red wine stains will sometimes remove or lighten them. Another method is to sprinkle salt on the stain and pour boiling water over it. Then launder the item using the hottest water possible, with chlorine bleach added along with the detergent. This may be a good time to return to the practice of using a corporal, a kind of place mat to protect the costly and often antique altar cloth. But the corporal should be something more absorbent than just another thin piece of linen, something with more substance like a plain, white, washable placemat. Plastic is unsuitable, not only because it looks tacky but also because it will not absorb spills or condensation. The inconspicuous corporal can be placed on the altar before the liturgy. It should be of useful size. If the cups are filled with wine on one side of the altar, then this, rather than or in addition to the center, may be the place for a corporal.

Candle drippings must be allowed to harden before they can be removed. First, with a dull knife, scrape away as much of the excess wax as possible. Then sandwich the wax spot between two pieces of paper toweling and iron with a hot iron, moving the toweling as the wax is absorbed. If there is a greasy residue, treat with a prewash spray and wash in hot water. If a dye stain remains from colored wax, sponge with one part alcohol to two parts water. Bleach will also take out any remaining stain.

The major cleaning problem with albs is perspiration stains, which tend to weaken fibers if allowed to remain in fabrics for any length of time. Always wash as promptly as possible. If colors have been transferred to the alb from another garment, try sponging fresh stains with ammonia, and use vinegar for older ones. Yellowed stains can be removed with bleach. If perspiration odor remains after the alb has been laundered, soak for an hour or more in warm water containing three or four tablespoons of salt for each quart of water.

The storage of these washable items is much the same as that for other liturgical textiles. Rolling altar cloths on acid-free tubes covered with acid-free tissue is the best method. After each wearing, albs should be hung where air can circulate freely, even if they are not damp or stained. Albs should be washed or dry cleaned (for the polyester-blended ones) regularly.

ABOUT THE AUTHORS AND ARTISTS

Katreen Bettencourt, born and raised in Belgium, began weaving liturgical vesture in 1964. She opened a studio in San Francisco in 1979 but now works in Cottage Grove, Oregon.

Connie Cassani Beard, a former art/design teacher, is a freelance graphic and textile designer. She lives in Colorado Springs.

Nancy Chinn is a painter and textile artist in Oakland, California. She is committed to creating art within and with a community, with members' active participation.

Vincent de Paul Crosby, OSB, a monk of St. Vincent Archabbey in Latrobe, Pennsylvania, is a vestment make and the director of Archabbey Studios, a service by which the abbey makes available to the wider church fine arts for use in worship.

John Dioszegi is a painter in Highland Park, Illinois.

Catherine Kapikian is a fiber artist and is artistic director of the Center for the Arts and Religion at Wesley Theological Seminary in Washington, D.C., a school of the Methodist church.

Judy Kensel Dioszegi's studio is in her home in Highland Park, Illinois. She designs and fabricates liturgical vesture in addition to creating banners, mobiles and fabric murals for churches, corporate atriums, hospitals, shopping malls, restaurants and private residences around the country.

Lynn Lautz is an art teacher and a designer/weaver of work for the liturgy. Her work is included in the archives of modern Christian art at the College of Notre Dame, Belmont, California.

David Philippart has a master's degree in liturgy from the University of Notre Dame and is the editor of *Environment & Art Letter*, Liturgy Training Publications' monthly magazine on church art and architecture.

G. Thomas Ryan, author of *The Sacristy Manual*, has a master's degree in liturgy from Catholic University of America.

Linda Schapper is a textile artist who specializes in quilts. She lives and works in Maitland, Florida.

Mark Scott is a teacher and artist in Forest Park, Illinois.

Mickey Wright is the research assistant in the department of textiles at the Art Institute of Chicago. She has a bachelor of fine arts in fiber from the School of the Art Institute and is completing a master of arts in modern art history (theory and criticism). She lives in Oak Park, Illinois, and does fiber art of her own.

Ronald John Zawilla, PHD, is the director of Gallery Genesis, Chicago, and a vestment maker.